THE CHURCH AT WORSHIP: CASE STUDIES FROM CHRISTIAN HIST...

Series Editors: LESTER RUTH, CARRIE STEENWYK, JOHN D. WITVLIET

Published

Walking Where Jesus Walked: Worship in Fourth-Century Jerusalem
  Lester Ruth, Carrie Steenwyk, John D. Witvliet

Tasting Heaven on Earth: Worship in Sixth-Century Constantinople
  Walter D. Ray

Forthcoming

Waiting in the Temple: Worship at a Black Holiness Church,
Early Twentieth Century
  Lester Ruth

Loving God Intimately: Worship with John Wimber
at Anaheim Vineyard Fellowship
  Andy Park, Lester Ruth, and Cindy Rethmeier

Tasting Heaven

on Earth

Worship in Sixth-Century Constantinople

WALTER D. RAY

William B. Eerdmans Publishing Company
Grand Rapids, Michigan / Cambridge, U.K.

Published 2012 by Wm. B. Eerdmans Publishing Co.

2140 Oak Industrial Drive N.E., Grand Rapids, Michigan 49505 /

P.O. Box 163, Cambridge CB3 9PU U.K.

Printed in the United States of America

17 16 15 14 13 12   7 6 5 4 3 2 1

Library of Congress Cataloging-in-Publication Data

Ray, Walter D.

  Tasting heaven on earth : worship in sixth-century Constantinople / Walter D. Ray.

    p. cm.   — (The church at worship)

  Includes index.

  ISBN 978-0-8028-6663-9 (pbk. : alk. paper)

  1. Public worship — Turkey — Istanbul. 2. Istanbul (Turkey) — Church history.   I. Title.

  BV6.R39 2012

  264'.01400949618 — dc23

                   2012006678

www.eerdmans.com

Contents

PART THREE: ASSISTING THE INVESTIGATION

Series Introduction

The Church at Worship offers user-friendly documentary case studies in the history of Christian worship. The series features a wide variety of examples, both prominent and obscure, from a range of continents, centuries, and Christian traditions. Whereas many historical studies of worship survey developments over time, offering readers a changing panoramic view like that offered out of an airplane window, each volume in *The Church at Worship* zooms in close to the surface, lingering over worship practices in a single time and place and allowing readers to sense the texture of specific worship practices in unique Christian communities. To complement books that study "the forest" of liturgical history, these volumes study "trees in the forest."

Each volume opens by orienting readers to the larger contexts of each example through a map, a timeline of events, and a summary of significant aspects of worship in the relevant time period and region. This section also includes any necessary cautions for the study of the particular case, as well as significant themes or practices to watch for while reading.

Each volume continues by focusing on the practices of worship in the specific case. This section begins with an introduction that explains the nature of participation in worship for ordinary worshipers. Many studies of worship have focused almost exclusively on what clergy do, say, and think. In contrast, insofar as historical sources allow it, this series focuses on the nature of participation of the entire community.

Each volume next presents an anthology of primary sources, presenting material according to the following categories: people and artifacts, worship setting and space, descriptions of worship, orders of service and texts, sermons, polity documents, and theology-of-worship documents. Each source is introduced briefly and is accompanied by a series of explanatory notes. Inclusion of these primary sources allows readers to have direct access to the primary material that historians draw upon for their summary descriptions and comparisons of practices. These sources are presented in ways that honor both academic rigor and accessibility. Our aim is to provide the best English editions of the resources possible, along with a complete set of citations that allow researchers to find quickly the best scholarly editions. At the same time, the introductory comments, explanatory sidebars, detailed glossaries, and devotional and small-group study questions make these volumes helpful not only for scholars and students but also for congregational study groups and a variety of other interested readers.

The presentation of sources attempts, insofar as it is possible, to take into account multiple disciplines of study related to worship. Worship is inevitably a multi-sensory experience, shaped by the sounds of words and music, the sight of symbols and spaces, the taste of bread and wine, and the fragrance of particular places and objects. Worship is also shaped by a variety of sources that never appear in the event itself: scriptural commands, theological treatises, and church polity rules or guidelines. In order to help readers sense this complex interplay, the volumes in this series provide a wide variety of texts and images. We particularly hope that this approach helps students of the history of preaching, architecture, and music, among others, to more deeply understand how their interests intersect with other disciplines.

Each volume concludes with suggestions for devotional use, study questions for congregational study groups, notes for students working in a variety of complementary disciplines, a glossary, suggestions for further study, works cited, and an index.

Students of Christian worship, church history, religious studies, and social or cultural history might use these case studies to complement the bird's-eye view offered by traditional textbook surveys.

Students in more specialized disciplines — including both liberal arts humanities (e.g., architectural or music history) and the subdisciplines of practical theology (e.g., evangelism, preaching, education, and pastoral care) — may use these volumes to discern how their own topic of interest interacts with worship practices. Liturgical music, church architecture, and preaching, for example, cannot be fully understood apart from a larger context of related practices.

This series is also written for congregational study groups, adult education classes, and personal study. It may be unconventional in some contexts to plan a congregational study group around original historical documents. But there is much to commend this approach. A reflective encounter with the texture of local practices in other times and places can be a profound act of discipleship. In the words of Andrew Walls, "Never before has the Church looked so much like the great multitude whom no one can number out of every nation and tribe and people and tongue. Never before, therefore, has there been so much potentiality for mutual enrichment and self-criticism, as God causes yet more light and truth to break forth from his word."[1]

This enrichment and self-criticism happens, in part, by comparing and contrasting the practices of another community with our own. As Rowan Williams explains, "Good history makes us think again about the definition of things we thought we understood pretty well, because it engages not just with what is familiar but with what is strange. It recognizes that 'the past is a foreign country' as well as being *our* past."[2] This is possible, in part, because of a theological conviction. As Williams points out, ". . . there is a sameness in the work of God. . . . We are not the first to walk this way; run your hand down the wood and the grain is

---

1. Andrew Walls, *The Missionary Movement in Christian History: Studies in the Transmission of Faith* (Maryknoll, N.Y.: Orbis Books, 1996), p. 15.

2. Rowan Williams, *Why Study the Past? The Quest for the Historical Church* (Grand Rapids: Wm. B. Eerdmans, 2005), p. 1.

still the same."[3] This approach turns on its head the minimalist perspective that "those who cannot remember the past are condemned to repeat it."[4] That oft-repeated truism implies that the goal of studying history is merely to avoid its mistakes. A more robust Christian sensibility is built around the conviction that the past is not just a comedy of errors but the arena in which God has acted graciously.

We pray that as you linger over this and other case studies in this series, you will be challenged and blessed through your encounter with one small part of the very large family of God. Near the end of his magisterial volume *A Secular Age,* Charles Taylor concludes, "None of us could ever grasp alone everything that is involved in our alienation from God and his action to bring us back. But there are a great many of us, scattered through history, who have had some powerful sense of some facet of this drama. Together we can live it more fully than any one of us could alone." What might this mean? For Taylor it means this: "Instead of reaching immediately for the weapons of polemic, we might better listen for a voice which we could never have assumed ourselves, whose tone might have been forever unknown to us if we hadn't *strained to understand it.* . . ."[5] We hope and pray that readers, eager to learn from worship communities across time and space, will indeed strain to understand what they find in these studies.

LESTER RUTH
Duke Divinity School
The Robert E. Webber Institute for Worship Studies

CARRIE STEENWYK
Calvin Institute of Christian Worship
Calvin College and Calvin Theological Seminary

JOHN D. WITVLIET
Calvin Institute of Christian Worship
Calvin College and Calvin Theological Seminary

3. Williams, *Why Study the Past?* p. 29.
4. George Santayana, *The Life of Reason* (New York: Scribner's, 1905), p. 284.
5. Charles Taylor, *A Secular Age* (Cambridge: Harvard University Press, 2007), p. 754.

Suggestions for Complementary Reading

For students of Christian worship wanting to survey the broader landscape, we recommend using the examples of these volumes alongside other books such as Geoffrey Wainwright and Karen B. Westerfield Tucker's *Oxford History of Christian Worship* (Oxford University Press, 2005); Gail Ramshaw's *Christian Worship: 100,000 Sundays of Symbols and Rituals* (Fortress Press, 2009); Marcel Metzger's *History of the Liturgy: The Major Stages,* translated by Madeleine Beaumont (Collegeville, Minn.: Liturgical Press, 1997); Frank C. Senn's *The People's Work: A Social History of the Liturgy* (Fortress Press, 2006) and *Christian Liturgy: Catholic and Evangelical* (Fortress Press, 1997); and James F. White's *Introduction to Christian Worship* (Abingdon Press, 2001), *A Brief History of Christian Worship* (Abingdon Press, 1993), and *Protestant Worship* (Westminster John Knox Press, 2006).

For those studying church history, volumes from this series might accompany volumes such as Mark Noll's *Turning Points: Decisive Moments in the History of Christianity* (Baker Academic, 2001) and Justo Gonzalez's *Church History: An Essential Guide* (Abingdon Press, 1996) and *The Story of Christianity,* vols. 1-2 (HarperOne, 1984 and 1985).

Students of religious studies might read these volumes alongside Robert A. Segal's *The Blackwell Companion to the Study of Religion* (Wiley-Blackwell, 2008) and John R. Hinnell's *The Routledge Companion to the Study of Religion* (Routledge, 2005).

History of music classes might explore the case studies of this series with Paul Westermeyer's *Te Deum: The Church and Music* (Augsburg Fortress Publishers, 1998) or Andrew Wilson-Dickson's *The Story of Christian Music: From Gregorian Chant to Black Gospel* (Augsburg Fortress Publishers, 2003).

History of preaching students might study the contextual examples provided in this series along with Hughes Oliphant Old's volumes of *The Reading and Preaching of the Scriptures in the Worship of the Christian Church* (Eerdmans, 1998-2007) or O. C. Edwards's *A History of Preaching* (Abingdon Press, 2004).

Acknowledgments

I am grateful to the many people who helped make this volume possible:

to Rachel Adams, Calvin Brondyke, Samantha Brondyke, Kyle Erffmeyer, Matt Gritter, Kent Hendricks, Shelley Veenstra Hendricks, Courtney Hexham, Rachel Klompmaker, Jana Kelder Koh, Brenda Janssen Kuyper, Anneke Leunk, Asher Mains, Becky Boender Ochsner, Kendra Pennings, Katie Roelofs, Katie Ritsema Roelofs, Eric Rottman, Annica Vander Linde, Bethany Meyer Vrieland, Tracie VerMerris Wiersma, Joanna Kooyenga Wigboldy, and Eric Zoodsma, whose work at the Calvin Institute of Christian Worship as student assistants has included hours of copying, scanning, typing, and other support for this volume;

to the editors, Lester Ruth of Duke Divinity School and Carrie Steenwyk and John Witvliet of the Calvin Institute of Christian Worship, for carefully reading each draft and providing invaluable input and direction, for tracking down sources and getting permissions, and for negotiating the publication process;

to teachers of liturgical history, especially Paul F. Bradshaw and Maxwell E. Johnson;

to liturgical scholars, especially Fr. Robert F. Taft, S.J., whose pioneering research on the history of Byzantine worship makes this volume possible, and the late Fr. Alexander Schmemann, whose insights into the liturgical mind of early Christians provide continuing inspiration;

to my mystagogues in Byzantine liturgy, especially Fr. Myron Manzuk and Paul Meyendorff;

to Hugh Claycombe for the production of two re-creations of worship space used in this volume;

to Hans Mast and Jim Forest for permission to include their photographs;

to the Lilly Endowment for financial support;

and to Mary Hietbrink and Tracey Gebbia for assistance in the publication process.

PART ONE

LOCATING THE WORSHIPING COMMUNITY

The Context of the Worshiping Community: Sixth-Century Constantinople

In the sixth century and for nine centuries more, Constantinople (ancient Byzantium, present-day Istanbul in Turkey) was the capital and principal city of the Roman Empire. It remains the spiritual homeland of hundreds of millions of Christians throughout the world who share a form of worship known as Byzantine. Separated from it for centuries by geography, culture, and history, most Western Christians have little understanding of this form of Christianity.

The story of Byzantine Christianity begins well before Constantine the Great, the first Christian Roman emperor, made the city his capital in 330 and renamed it New Rome or Constantinople. Byzantium was located less than two miles across the Bosporus Strait from the Roman province of Bithynia, whose Christians the apostle Peter addressed in his First Epistle, and not far from the area of Paul's missionary activity. It is likely that a Christian community was established in Byzantium in the apostolic or immediate post-apostolic period. By the end of the second century, the Christians of Byzantium had already experienced persecution. As the stature of the city increased within the empire, so did the authority of its church and **bishop**, the chief clergyperson in a church or region.

In less than a century after Constantine's conversion in 312, Christianity went from a persecuted religion to the official religion of the empire. The emperor became responsible for the proper ordering of the church, even in matters of worship and theology. (See Justinian's decrees on pp. 133-34.) The emperor's church in Constantinople often found itself in the middle of doctrinal controversy. For example, to promote church unity in 325, Constantine called the Council of Nicea to deal with the question of Christ's divinity. The council condemned the **presbyter** Arius and his followers, the **Arians**, for teaching that Christ was less than God. This council set a precedent for the further involvement of the emperor (or empress) in church matters.

In this volume, *presbyter* refers to the next rank of clergy beneath the bishop.

By the sixth century, the issue was not only the divinity of Christ but also his humanity. Two councils had been held to deal with this issue, at **Ephesus** in 431 and at **Chalcedon** in 451. The first affirmed for the Virgin Mary the title of **Theotokos** ("God-bearer" or, less accurately, "Mother of God"), a title popular in the worship of Constantinople but challenged by **Nestorius** when he became archbishop there in 428. Nestorius argued that Mary gave birth only to the man Jesus. Ephesus rejected the ideas of Nestorius as making too great a separation between the divine and human natures in Christ. The **Council of Chalcedon** tried

3

to respond to the opposite problem of not making a great enough distinction between the natures. It produced a more precise statement of their relationship: "We confess one and the same our Lord Jesus Christ . . . acknowledged in two natures without confusion, without change, without division, without separation . . . combining in one person and hypostasis — not divided or separated into two persons, but one and the same Son and only-begotten God, Logos, Lord Jesus Christ."[1]

Chalcedon did not end the controversy. Most of the church of Alexandria in Egypt and much of the Syrian church rejected the two-nature formula of Chalcedon in favor of the formula of Cyril of Alexandria (d. 436), which recognized "one incarnate nature of God the Word." So, for a while, did the imperial church in Constantinople. Non-Chalcedonian theologians, pejoratively known as **Monophysites** ("One nature" people), wanted to make clear that the Word of God himself was the one who was born, died, and rose from the dead. For the people of the time, it was a matter of life and death. If God had not fully assumed human life and if divine life was not fully accessible to humans, there could be no salvation.

Ongoing dialogue with non-Chalcedonian theology played a more important role in the church of Constantinople than in the churches in the West. Doctrinal controversy left its mark on Constantinople's worship. One result was the recitation in Sunday worship of the Nicene Creed, which had been cited at Chalcedon. First used by non-Chalcedonians when they were in the ascendancy in Constantinople, to show that they were as orthodox as Chalcedon, it was retained when the Chalcedonian party took control in 518 with Emperor Justin I. Another addition during this period was the hymn "The Only-Begotten" (or **Ho Monogenes**; see p. 86), which the emperor Justinian I introduced,[2] and perhaps composed himself, as an appeal to non-Chalcedonian theology. The hymn affirmed that the immortal Word of God, one of the Trinity, became incarnate "without change" and was crucified for us.

In the fifth and sixth centuries, the veneration of Mary gained prominence as a way of affirming the truth of the Incarnation. (See Romanos's **kontakion** on the Nativity, pp. 105-12, for an example of reflection on the Incarnation through contemplation of Mary's role in it.) During these centuries, new feasts of Mary joined her commemoration on December 26 in the Byzantine church calendar.

As the church of the emperor, the church of Constantinople naturally incorporated imperial ceremony into its worship. At the same time, Byzantine worship reflected the developing understanding of the role of the emperor in the church. Both processes can be seen in the rite of the emperor's entrance, which was prescribed for certain feast days. (See the entrance of Justinian and Theodora in the mosaics on p. 33.) The emperor, removing his crown, entered the church with the bishop preceded by a **deacon** carrying the Gospel book. The Gospel was

The Arab invasions of the seventh century removed most of the non-Chalcedonian churches from the Roman Empire, forestalling further dialogue. Renewed dialogue in the twentieth century led to a broad consensus among Eastern churches. A commission of bishops and theologians from both families of churches affirmed that "both families have always loyally maintained the same authentic Orthodox Christological faith and the unbroken continuity of the apostolic tradition, though they have used Christological terms in different ways" (Joint Commission of the Theological Dialogue between the Orthodox and Oriental Orthodox Churches, "Second Agreed Statement," Geneva, 1990).

A kontakion is a long hymn or hymnic sermon consisting of 18 to 24 stanzas composed around a theme.

Deacons, an order of ministry below that of presbyters, lead the people's prayers, keep order in the church, assist with communion, and perform other similar tasks.

1. Cited from Jaroslav Pelikan, *The Christian Tradition: A History of the Development of Doctrine,* vol. 1: *The Emergence of the Catholic Tradition* (Chicago and London: University of Chicago Press, 1971), pp. 263-64.

2. Hugh Wybrew, *The Orthodox Liturgy: The Development of the Eucharistic Liturgy in the Byzantine Rite* (Crestwood, N.Y.: St. Vladimir's Seminary Press, 1990), p. 111.

enthroned on the **altar table**, while the emperor, having laid his gift of gold or silver on the altar, assumed his throne in the **nave**, the central part of the church between aisles. Although the Eastern Church was willing to give the emperor the initiative even in matters of doctrine, there was a limit to the extent it would follow him. More often than not, the church rejected what the emperor proposed, as was clear already in the fourth century when it rejected the Arianism of Constantine's sons. The limit was defined by the truth of the Gospel, before which the emperor removed his crown and took his place with the people.[3]

Because of its status as the church of the capital, the worship of the Great Church of Constantinople became a model for other churches. Eventually, Constantinople's worship supplanted that of the other Eastern churches in communion with it. Today this form of worship remains the **rite** of the Eastern Orthodox and Byzantine-rite Catholics.

The altar table is the table on which the bread and wine for communion are consecrated.

3. Observant readers will notice that Emperor Justinian and Empress Theodora are wearing crowns in the entrance procession depicted in the sixth-century Ravenna mosaics (pp. 32-33). The tenth-century *On the Ceremonies of the Byzantine Court* says that the crown is removed from the emperor's head as he enters the narthex of the church and replaced on his head, by the patriarch himself, only as he is leaving the church after the service. This discrepancy points to the limitations of our sources. It is possible that the ritual changed between the sixth and the tenth centuries. On the other hand, in accordance with (mostly unwritten) iconographic standards, icons always show emperors and empresses wearing their crowns so they can be identified. See the discussion in Thomas F. Mathews, *The Early Churches of Constantinople: Architecture and Liturgy* (University Park: Pennsylvania State University, 1971), p. 147.

Timeline

What was happening in the world?

ca. 280: The future emperor Constantine I is born.

285: The Roman Empire is divided into East and West.

312: Constantine leads his army to victory over rival Maxentius and attributes his success to Christ.

324: Constantine reunites the Roman Empire and becomes sole emperor.

330: Byzantium is made the capital of the Roman Empire, being renamed New Rome or Constantinople.

337: Emperor Constantine I dies; the Roman Empire is divided between his sons.

354-56: Germanic peoples invade Gaul.

ca. 360-70: Huns invade Europe.

395: After the death of Theodosius I, the Roman Empire is permanently divided into East and West.

What was happening in Christianity?

301: King Tiridates III of Armenia converts to Christianity, making Armenia the first Christian nation.

325: The First Council of Nicea, the first general council of the church, affirms the deity of Christ, sets the date for the celebration of Easter, gives norms on liturgy, and formulates the Nicene Creed; disputes over the creed continue in the East until 381.

340-439: Persian Christians suffer intense persecution.

340: The conversion of King Ezana makes Ethiopia the second Christian nation.

379-95: During the reign of Theodosius I, the Roman Empire officially becomes a Christian state.

381: The First Council of Constantinople, the second general council of the church, solidifies orthodox statements on the Persons of the Trinity. This ends disputes over Nicea.

What was happening in the Church of Constantinople?

330: The dedication of Constantinople is celebrated in its newly restored Church of Holy Peace (Hagia Eirene).

337-81: The Roman emperors mainly oppose the Nicene Creed; there is a strong anti-Nicene influence in the Church of Constantinople.

360: The Church of Holy Wisdom (Hagia Sophia) is dedicated during the reign of Constantius II, son of Constantine.

379-81: Gregory Nazianzen, bishop of Constantinople, preaches in a house church he calls the Anastasis (Resurrection) because he is resurrecting Constantinople for Nicene Orthodoxy.

381: The First Council of Constantinople recognizes the Church of Constantinople, "New Rome," as second in honor after the Church of Old Rome.

398: John Chrysostom, a priest from Antioch renowned for his preaching, becomes **patriarch** (the title given to the bishops of certain important Christian centers) of Constantinople.

What was happening in the world?	What was happening in Christianity?	What was happening in the Church of Constantinople?
		404: Chrysostom is banished for a second time because of political and ecclesiastical intrigue; Hagia Sophia is razed in subsequent riots.
409: The Vandals take Spain. 410: Rome is sacked by the Visigoths under Alaric.	410-40: Pope Leo I presides over the church of Rome.	415: The second Church of Hagia Sophia is dedicated.
428-30: The Vandals take North Africa.	424: The Persian church declares independence from the church in the Roman Empire.	428: Nestorius, a priest from Antioch, becomes patriarch of Constantinople and sparks controversy by preaching against calling Mary *Theotokos* ("Birth-giver of God"), drawing opposition from Cyril, patriarch of Alexandria.
	431: The **Council of Ephesus**, the third general council, affirms the title *Theotokos* for Mary, arguing that Christ's divinity cannot be separated from his humanity. Ephesus is eventually rejected by the Church of the East in Persia.	431: The Council of Ephesus deposes Nestorius.
476: Ravenna, the last capital of the Western Roman Empire, falls to the Heruli.	451: The Council of Chalcedon, the fourth general council, defines the two-nature doctrine of Christ. The council is rejected by large segments of the churches of Alexandria and Antioch, and later by the Ethiopian and Armenian churches, beginning the separation of "non-Chalcedonian" churches.	451: The Council of Chalcedon gives the bishop of Constantinople jurisdiction over the provinces of Thrace, Asia, and Pontus.
482: Justinian, the future emperor, is born.	482: Emperor Zeno, along with Patriarch Acacius, issues the *Henotikon*, or "formula of union," to reconcile the non-Chalcedonian churches; the formula is rejected by the pope of Rome.	484: Pope Felix III of Rome excommunicates Patriarch Acacius over the *Henotikon;* Acacius, in turn, excommunicates Felix, beginning a schism with Rome. 511-12: Religious riots erupt over Emperor Anastasius's attempt to introduce a non-Chalcedonian phrase into the entrance hymn of the liturgy.

What was happening in the world?	What was happening in Christianity?	What was happening in the Church of Constantinople?
518-27: Justin I, uncle of Justinian, reigns as Roman emperor.		ca. 518: The deacon Romanos, known as the Melodist, begins his hymn-writing career in Constantinople.
		519: Emperor Justin I, with help from his nephew Justinian, restores communion with Rome.
527-65: Justinian I reigns as Roman emperor.		
529: The Code of Justinian, a compilation of Roman laws that will become the basis for the later Western legal system, is published.	529: Justinian closes the last pagan university, that of Athens.	
532: The Nika Revolt by circus factions threatens Justinian's rule and is violently suppressed.		532: Hagia Sophia is burned down in the Nika Revolt; rebuilding begins.
533: Concluding a peace treaty with Persia after five years of war, Justinian sets his sights on the reconquest of the Western Empire.		
534: North Africa is recaptured from the Vandals.		
		535-36: Justinian introduces the hymn "Only-Begotten" into the liturgy in an attempt to reconcile non-Chalcedonians.
537: Rome is retaken from the Goths.		537: The third, domed Church of Hagia Sophia is dedicated.
540: Ravenna, the last capital of the Western Empire, is recaptured from the Goths; the same year, Chosroes (or Khosrau) I of Persia sacks Antioch in the East.		542: Bubonic plague kills 300,000 people in Constantinople, up to 40 percent of the population.
	544: To placate non-Chalcedonians, Justinian issues a decree condemning the "Three Chapters," certain writings tending toward Nestorianism; Pope Vigilius takes the decree as an attack on Chalcedon.	
545: Rome falls again to Totila the Goth.	545: Pope Vigilius is forcibly brought to Constantinople.	545-53: Pope Vigilius resides in Constantinople, negotiating with Justinian over the "Three Chapters."
552: The Italian peninsula is retaken for the Empire.	553: The Second Council of Constantinople, the fifth general council, condemns the "Three Chapters"; Pope Vigilius agrees.	552-65: Eutychius is patriarch of Constantinople. When he opposes Justinian's later flirtation with a non-Chalcedonian theology, he is arrested and exiled.
556: Persia agrees to a fifty-year peace treaty.		557: An earthquake destroys the dome of Hagia Sophia, which is rebuilt with a stronger design.
562: The Avars invade Thrace, west of the capital.		562: The restored Hagia Sophia is rededicated.
565: Justinian I dies.		

What was happening in the world?

565-78: Justin II reigns as Roman emperor.

567: The Lombards invade and capture the central Italian peninsula.

571: War resumes with Persia after Justin withholds tribute promised by Justinian.

577: Slavs invade and hold Thrace and Illyricum, the northern Balkans, and push into the Greek peninsula.

610-41: Heraclius reigns as Roman emperor.

611: Persia captures Antioch.

613: Persia captures Damascus.

614: Persia captures Jerusalem.

626-27: Heraclius definitively defeats the Persian army in Mesopotamia, recovering the True Cross and relics of the Passion.

632: Mohammed dies.

633: Arab armies begin the conquest of Syria.

637: Arab armies take Jerusalem.

640: Arab armies conquer Egypt.

What was happening in Christianity?

580-662: Maximus the Confessor lives. He begins his career as a court official in Constantinople and later becomes a monastic leader and the chief opponent of the idea of Monotheletism proposed by Emperor Heraclius I.

590-610: Gregory I is pope of Rome.

614: Persians take the True Cross (believed to be the cross on which Christ was crucified) and other relics of the Passion as spoils from Jerusalem.

622-41: To reconcile non-Chalcedonians, Heraclius promotes **Monotheletism**, the idea that Christ has only one will (*thelema*). The idea is opposed by Sophronius of Jerusalem, Maximus the Confessor, and Pope Martin I of Rome; it is condemned at the Third Council of Constantinople, the sixth general council, in 680.

629: The True Cross is returned to Jerusalem.

640: With the fall of Egypt, all non-Chalcedonian churches are effectively removed from the Roman Empire, foreclosing any further attempts at reconciliation.

What was happening in the Church of Constantinople?

577-82: When Patriarch John Scholasticus dies, the people demand that Eutychius be returned from exile and become patriarch again.

588: Patriarch John the Faster assumes the title "Ecumenical" (i.e., "of the whole inhabited world"); the title is reluctantly accepted by Rome after initial opposition by Popes Pelagius and Gregory I.

626: Persians, Slavs, and Avars besiege Constantinople and are driven back, the people believe, by the intercessions of the Virgin Mary, whose **icon** had been paraded around the walls of the city every day of the siege.

628: Heraclius's triumphant return to the capital on September 14 culminates in the elevation of the True Cross in Hagia Sophia; the date becomes a permanent feast in the Byzantine calendar.

Liturgical Landscape

What liturgical worlds surrounded Constantinople in the sixth century? If a Constantinopolitan worshiper looked around, what might she see?

From the peace of Constantine in the fourth century, when the church began to be organized along the administrative boundaries of the Roman Empire, there began to emerge families of rites, usually based in geographic regions and centered in major administrative centers such as Antioch, Alexandria, Jerusalem, Rome, and Milan. Worship within a region bore a "family resemblance" on the basis of related texts and common practices. The Sunday Lord's Supper service in all these families shared a basic structural division of two parts: the first devoted to readings from the Bible and the sermon, the second to prayers and communion. But they differed in their selection and number of Bible readings, in the text of their prayers, in their use of psalms and hymns, and in their arrangement and use of liturgical space. The rites also differed from place to place in how they organized time, the number and content of daily services, and the feasts celebrated in the church calendar. For overviews of the different families, see Frank C. Senn, *Christian Liturgy: Catholic and Evangelical* (Minneapolis: Fortress Press, 1997), pp. 115-46; and the entries on liturgical traditions in *The New Dictionary of Sacramental Worship,* ed. Peter Fink (Collegeville, Minn.: Liturgical Press, 1990).

Constantinopolitans could have become aware of many of these liturgical traditions from visitors and immigrants to the city. The liturgy of Antioch was the most familiar, since the Constantinople rite was a member of Antioch's family of rites. In the fourth and fifth centuries, several of Constantinople's bishops came from Antioch or Asia Minor. Knowledge of Jerusalem's liturgy, with its special practices associated with sites from the life of Christ, came back with the many pilgrims to the Holy Land. The Syrian church's tradition of liturgical poetry came to Constantinople with the immigrant deacon and hymn writer Romanos the Melodist. In Syriac-speaking areas, even sermons were composed in verse. The most famous verse homilies are those of the fourth-century Ephrem of Syria.

The worshipers of Constantinople would have been very aware of the elaborate ceremony of the imperial court. This ceremony was both a rival to and a model for the liturgy of the church. The emperor was the most prominent worshiper of the city, which meant that elements of the imperial ceremony had to be incorporated into the liturgy. For a description of the impact of imperial ceremony on the development of the Byzantine liturgy, especially in the **Cathedral Church** of Holy Wisdom (best known by its Greek name, Hagia Sophia; also called the Great Church as the cathedral church of the imperial capital), see Robert F. Taft,

A Cathedral Church is the church in which a bishop is considered to have his residence or "seat" *(kathedra).*

10

"The Byzantine Rite Becomes Imperial," chapter 3 in *The Byzantine Rite: A Short History* (Collegeville, Minn.: Liturgical Press, 1992).

Theological controversies also helped to shape liturgy. In these controversies the emperor sought to hold the church together, and all sides sought to gain the ear of the emperor. All the theological tendencies, along with their liturgical manifestations, were represented in Constantinople as the imperial capital. In the fifth century, John Chrysostom instituted liturgical processions through the streets of Constantinople for his church to counter similar processions of the rival Arian churches. In the sixth century, too, the liturgical practices of rival groups, especially the non-Chalcedonian churches, influenced the liturgy of the Great Church, the city's main church of Hagia Sophia. For the development of the **stational** (processional) **liturgy** of Constantinople, see John Baldovin, *The Urban Character of Christian Worship: The Origins, Development, and Meaning of Stational Liturgy,* Orientalia Christiana Analecta 228 (Rome: Pont. Institutum Studiorum Orientalium, 1987). For an account of disturbances that took place in Constantinople at the beginning of the sixth century over attempts to introduce non-Chalcedonian practices into the liturgy of the Great Church, see John Julius Norwich, *Byzantium: The Early Centuries* (New York: Alfred A. Knopf, 1996), pp. 184-87.

Monasteries played a significant role in the capital. In the sixth century, there were over seventy monasteries in Constantinople. By the tenth century, monks and nuns comprised up to 10 percent of the city's population. Monasteries had their own liturgical traditions. Although monastic liturgy did not directly affect the liturgy of the Great Church until after **Iconoclasm** (the imperial effort to stop the use of **icons** in churches in the eighth and ninth centuries), it did influence popular piety, especially perhaps the rule of prayer of the *akoimetai* ("sleepless") monasteries, in which prayers and praise were raised to God around the clock. On the role of monastics in Byzantine society, see Cyril Mango, "Saints," in *The Byzantines,* edited by Guglielmo Cavallo, translated by Thomas Dunlap, Teresa Lavender Fagan, and Charles Lambert (Chicago and London: University of Chicago Press, 1997), pp. 255-80.

Icon comes from the Greek word for image. Icons are used to decorate churches and as a focus of veneration.

Geographical Landscape

Constantinople, modern-day Istanbul, is located on a peninsula on the western side of the Bosporus Strait, the boundary between Europe and Asia. In the sixth century, Constantinople was the leading city and capital of the Roman Empire.

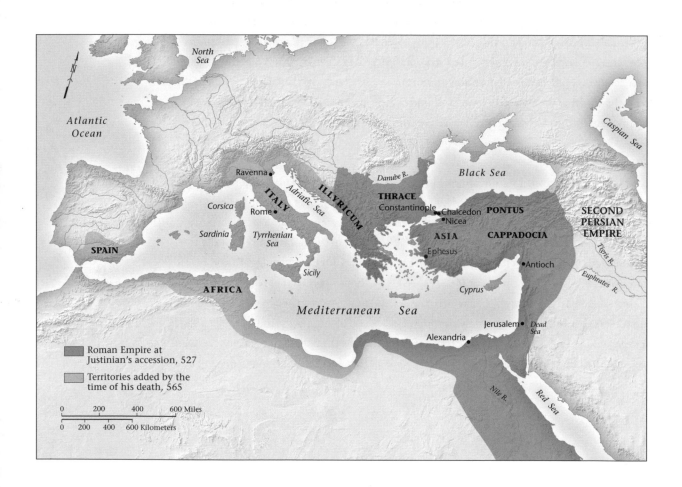

Roman Empire at Justinian's accession, 527

Territories added by the time of his death, 565

Cautions for Studying Constantinople's Worship History

These are some of the methodological difficulties about which a reader should be aware when studying Constantinople's worship.

- There is an absence of surviving liturgical documents from the period. The earliest surviving manuscript of the Byzantine Eucharistic liturgy comes from the late eighth century. The tricky thing is determining what elements in this manuscript carry over from earlier stages of the liturgy and whether and how they have changed in the intervening years. To answer these questions, we are forced to work back from later existing texts, relying on the liturgical commentaries of Maximus the Confessor (early seventh century; see p. 49) and Germanus of Constantinople (early eighth century), on imperial regulations and church canons that impinged upon the liturgy (see pp. 133ff.), and on sermons from the time (see "Sermons," pp. 105ff.). Popular accounts of lives of the saints also provide glimpses of worship practices.
- There is also a similar absence of prescriptive texts for the imperial ceremony. We must rely on eyewitness descriptions, on a tenth-century work by Emperor Constantine VII Porphyrogenitus, *On the Ceremonies of the Byzantine Court,* which appears to be compiled from earlier sources, and on artworks from the period, such as the mosaics in Ravenna showing the imperial entrance (see pp. 32-33).
- The original liturgical furnishings of Hagia Sophia have been lost. We must reconstruct what Hagia Sophia looked like through eyewitness descriptions of sixth-century writers, such as Procopius and Paul the Silentiary (see pp. 66-69 and pp. 70-81), through careful examination of the building in its present state, and through comparison with the remains of other churches of Constantinople.
- The original artwork in Hagia Sophia and other churches has been lost, and there is a scarcity of reflection from the period on the role that art played in the worship and spiritual life of Christians. Only about seventy icons remain from before Iconoclasm, the period in the eighth and ninth centuries during which the destruction of religious images was official imperial policy. Artwork and other products of material culture, such as liturgical implements, can provide clues to the way liturgy was seen and experienced (see pp. 29-36).
- Some of the most historically accurate descriptions are also some of the briefest, since

the primary goal of these ancient sources was not to describe worship practices. For example, the lives of saints sometimes drop in a detail or two about liturgy that are trustworthy because liturgy is not the main concern of these works. Conversely, the ancient, lengthy descriptions of church buildings (e.g., pp. 66-69 and pp. 70-81) should be considered not technical architectural records but idealized portrayals based on what the authors perceived the spiritual significance of the buildings to be.

- Some people have misconceptions about the unchanging quality of Eastern Orthodox worship. The Eastern churches' first centuries were times of great creativity. The Church of Constantinople never stopped developing its liturgy. Especially after Iconoclasm in the ninth century, the Byzantine liturgy accepted significant influence from the liturgies of monasteries in Constantinople and Jerusalem, a process that continued into the fourteenth century. As the Byzantine rite was adopted by regions far from Constantinople, it was translated into various languages and adapted to the needs and circumstances of the people using it.

Significant Themes and Practices to Observe

As you study the following materials, be on the lookout for these significant themes and practices, which are categorized by some of the primary elements in the practice of worship.

Piety

- The church saw its worship as participating in the angelic, heavenly worship of God.
- The presence of the imperial court flavored the worship of the city's churches, including the use of imperial ritual to adore the exalted Christ.
- The Church of Constantinople used worship as a way both to counter and to co-opt lingering pagan customs and sentiments.

Time

- Like heaven, the worship in Constantinople might have seemed unending. Regular rounds of daily and weekly worship were supplemented by many special services.
- Special feast days throughout the year marked events in the life of Christ and commemorated Mary and the saints.

Place

- The size, construction, and beauty of the main church, Hagia Sophia, created a sense of both God's transcendence and God's immanence.
- Movement into and through the worship space was an important part of worship and carried part of the meaning of the service. The people felt as if they ascended into heaven.
- Processions through the city to the appointed church of the day turned the whole city into a worship space and emphasized that all the Christians of the city belonged to one church.

Prayer

- Prayer was the principal act of worship of the baptized faithful.

- The prayers frequently remembered God's saving activity, often portrayed as dramatic and decisive for the world's redemption.
- The service was saturated with prayer: prayers of various kinds were repeated throughout the order of worship.
- The focus of the Lord's Supper service was thanksgiving, the central act of which was the Great Prayer of Thanksgiving, also known as the Eucharistic prayer or **anaphora**.
- The intercessions had a breadth appropriate to the Risen Lord, who redeems the whole cosmos.

Preaching

- Sermons were based on the Bible readings assigned to the day.
- Rather than providing detailed explanations of an isolated Bible text, early Orthodox preaching proclaimed the effect of God's saving acts in large, bold strokes. They showed how the passage fit into the larger picture of God's plan of salvation.
- Sermons invited the hearers to compare their lives with those of the biblical characters and to see themselves as part of God's ongoing plan.

Music

- Psalms provided many of the important song texts but were supplemented with several important, popular hymns.
- Psalms and hymns were used to accompany liturgical processions through the city and in the church.
- The use of short refrains allowed the congregation to join in between the verses sung by a cantor or choir.

People

- The bishop was the chief worship leader in the main Eucharistic services. The bishop of Constantinople was one of the most important in the Eastern Empire and was given the title "patriarch."
- Several orders of clergy, each with its own worship responsibilities, assisted the bishop. The laity also had responsibilities in worship.
- The stratification of society was reflected in who used which space in Hagia Sophia.
- The emperor and empress were the most visible worshipers of the city and often played a prominent role in the service.

PART TWO

EXPLORING THE WORSHIPING COMMUNITY

Describing the Community's Worship: Constantinople in the Sixth Century

What follows is a description of worship as it might have occurred in Hagia Sophia, the main church in Constantinople (present-day Istanbul) in the middle of the sixth century. This reconstruction is pieced together from a variety of sources, especially early descriptions of the wonder of this building, a few descriptions of worship from the period, and the earliest worship books available. Of particular importance is how Christian worship and its use of space can give awareness of participation in God's plan of salvation.

Hagia Sophia, interior, 19th-century lithograph. See p. 38 for more details.

Heaven on earth. That's how the sixth-century worshiper experienced the newly rebuilt Church of Holy Wisdom (Hagia Sophia, the Great Church) in Constantinople. "Whenever anyone enters this church to pray," writes the sixth-century historian Procopius (see p. 68), "... his mind is lifted up toward God and exalted, feeling that God cannot be far away.... And this does not happen only to one who sees the church for the first time, but the same experience comes to him on each successive occasion, as though the sight were new each time."[1] Four centuries later, visitors from Kievan Rus', ancestors of the modern Ukrainians and Russians, had the same feeling. "The Greeks led us into the edifices where they worship their God, and we knew not whether we were in heaven or on earth. For on earth there is no such splendor or such beauty, and we are at a loss how to describe it. We know only that God dwells there among men."[2] To early Byzantine worshipers, it must have seemed that the Scripture was fulfilled among them: the transcendent God had come to dwell in the midst of his people. The **Kingdom of God** was at hand.

The Kingdom of God is a New Testament image for the fullness of salvation at the end of or beyond time that is frequently found in Byzantine liturgical texts.

1. Procopius of Caesarea, *Buildings*, trans. H. B. Dewing, I.i.61-62, vol. 7 of *Procopius*, Loeb Classical Library (Cambridge, Mass.: Harvard University Press/London: William Heinemann, 1954).
2. *Russian Primary Chronicle*, in *Medieval Russia's Epics, Chronicles, and Tales*, ed. Serge A. Zenkovsky (New York: Dutton, 1964), pp. 67-68.

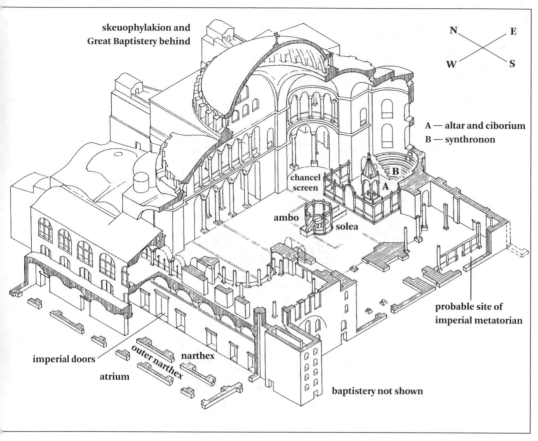

skeuophylakion and
Great Baptistery behind

N

E

W

S

A — altar and ciborium
B — synthronon

chancel
screen

B

A

ambo

solea

probable site of
imperial metatorian

imperial doors

outer narthex

narthex

atrium

baptistery not shown

**Cutaway view of
Hagia Sophia.**

Source: Rowland J.
Mainstone, *Hagia
Sophia: Architecture,
Structure, and Liturgy
of Justinian's Great
Church* (New York:
Thames & Hudson,
1988), image 252 on
p. 233.

Rebuilt by the emperor Justinian after an earlier church was burned down during riots in 532, Hagia Sophia impressed worshipers with its immense size and beauty. At the time it was built, it was the largest enclosed space in the world. A football field in length and two-thirds as wide, the church ascended in a series of curves and arches and culminated in a dome 100 feet wide and 180 feet above the ground, the height of an eighteen-story building. To Procopius, the roof "seems not to rest on solid masonry, but to cover the space with its golden dome suspended from heaven."[3]

The floor plan was that of a wide **basilica**, a rectangle with its long axis running approximately west to east. The open central space, or **nave**, was separated from side aisles to the north and south by the piers supporting the central dome and columns supporting galleries or balconies more than forty feet above the floor. At the front of the church, in the eastern end, was an **apse** (a semicircular area on the eastern end of a basilica) in which was located the **synthronon**, the bishop's throne, composed of seven large semicircular masonry steps rising to a height of about fifteen feet. The top step held silver seats for the bishop and presbyters. From this height they were able to look over their audience while they preached.

Hagia Sophia was furnished like other churches in the capital. In the center of the nave was an **ambo**, an oval-shaped raised platform from which Scripture was read. Paul the Silentiary, another sixth-century author (see p. 70), describes the ambo as an island in a sea of thronging people. The ambo in Hagia Sophia was supported by eight columns and accessed

---

3. Procopius, *Building*, I.i.46-47.

from the east and from the west by flights of seven stairs. Beneath the ambo stood the cantors who led the congregation in the psalmody between the Bible readings, during the procession with the bread and wine, and at communion. From the steps of the ambo, the deacons would lead the prayers of the faithful and give commands: "Stand up!" "Wisdom! Let us pay attention!" "Guard the doors!" "Let us pray!"

The deacons' commands were not just part of the ritual. One of their duties was to maintain order in the church. There were no pews. The people did not stand stationary; they took an active part in the service. Paul the Silentiary, continuing with his maritime imagery, tells us that, as the Gospel book was carried from the ambo to the altar after the Bible readings, "the surging crowd strives to touch the sacred book with their lips and hands, while moving waves of people break around."[4] To keep the crowds from hindering the ministers in their liturgical activities, low marble barriers were used to set aside spaces for the liturgy, an elliptical one around the ambo and a square or "π"-shaped one surrounding three sides of the altar table, which sat in the nave just in front of the eastern apse. A walkway called the **solea** led from the ambo to the altar area, which was called the **sanctuary**.

The altar table of Hagia Sophia was made of bronze and covered in gold and silver leaf. In the sixth century, it was covered by an altar cloth embroidered with images: on the front was Christ flanked by Peter and Paul, and on the sides were its donors, Emperor Justinian and Empress Theodora, shown joining hands with Christ and Mary. Above the altar was a **ciborium**, a roof-like structure supported by four columns. The barrier around the altar was topped by twelve columns supporting a beam or **architrave** covered with silver into which were worked images of Christ, Mary, angels, and apostles. A similar architrave on columns topped the barrier around the ambo.

Completing the visual effect was the light flooding in through windows, forty of them around the base of the dome alone. Describing the church, Procopius writes, "It is bathed in sunlight and the reflection of the sun's rays; one might almost say that it is not illuminated from without by the sun, but that the radiance originates from within, so inundated with light is this sanctuary."[5] The light reflected off the marble of the walls, the gold mosaic which covered the dome, and the gold and silver of the furnishings. Even at night, a multitude of lamps made it appear as if, in the words of Paul the Silentiary, "some nocturnal sun filled the majestic temple with light. . . . Thus the bright night smiles like the day and appears herself to be rosy-ankled. . . ."[6]

Hagia Sophia was a symbol of Constantinople's vision of itself, the Christian capital of

In Byzantine sources the "altar" or sanctuary refers to the whole area around the table where the bread and wine are consecrated. What we might now call the altar is called "the table" or "holy table," recalling the meal in which the Eucharist originated, Christ's Last Supper.

In the age of the electric light, we may forget the symbolic power of the rhythmic alternation of light and dark. But for the early Christians, light was an important symbol meaning life (John 1:4-5), salvation (Luke 2:29-32; 1 Peter 2:9), the Kingdom of God (Col. 1:12-13), God's glory (Matt. 17:2; Rev. 21:23), God (1 John 1:5; Rev. 22:5), and Christ (John 1:9, 8:12, etc.). Like other early Christian worship traditions, Byzantine liturgy made full use of this symbolism. The daily moments of change from daylight to darkness and darkness to daylight were marked by services of psalms, hymns, and prayers. Prayer was made toward the coming light, so churches were built to face the east. The Eucharist was generally celebrated in the morning, when light poured in from behind the sanctuary. Hagia Sophia was designed to make maximum use of light.

4. Paulus Silentiarius, *Descr. S. Ambonis,* 240; quoted by Hugh Wybrew in *The Orthodox Liturgy: The Development of the Eucharistic Liturgy in the Byzantine Rite* (Crestwood, N.Y.: St. Vladimir's Seminary Press, 1990), pp. 73-74.

5. Procopius, *Buildings,* I.i.30, quoted by Wybrew in *The Orthodox Liturgy,* p. 80.

6. Paulus Silentiarius, *Descr. S. Sophiae,* 806, 884, in Cyril Mango, *The Art of the Byzantine Empire, 312-1453: Sources and Documents* (Englewood Cliffs, N.J.: Prentice Hall, 1972).

Hagia Sophia, interior. Morning light streams through the dome and apse of Hagia Sophia. See p. 39 for details.

Source: Erich Lessing/ Art Resource, NY

a Christian empire. Since the conversion of Constantine and the establishment of Constantinople as the capital of the Roman Empire in the fourth century, the city had been becoming more consciously Christian. If they were born in Constantinople, residents might call themselves Byzantine, from the ancient name for their city, Byzantium. They would all call themselves Roman, for the empire of which their city was the capital. But increasingly, their primary term of self-identification was simply Christian.[7] They believed that their city and its empire were part of God's "plan for the fullness of time, to unite all things in Christ" (Eph. 1:10). Their empire was to be the manifestation of God's Kingdom. They did not, however, equate the empire with this Kingdom. The empire was to be the witness to the Kingdom of God, an image or icon in the present age of the age to come. Byzantine Christians expected the second coming of Christ and an end to this present age. It was their job to hasten this end by making "this gospel of the Kingdom" known "throughout the whole world, as a testimony to all nations" (Matt. 24:14; see the way Maximus the Confessor uses this verse in *The Church's Mystagogy,* chapter 14, p. 56).[8]

To the sixth-century inhabitants of Constantinople, it may have seemed that the end was near. Justinian was succeeding in his plan to re-unite the eastern and western parts of the empire. (In the fifth century, the West had been lost to Goths and Germanic tribes.) Elsewhere, Christian missionaries were having success. The sixth-century traveler Cosmas Indicopleustes (Cosmas, "Voyager to India") reported that from India in the East to Spain in the West and from the Ethiopians in the South to the Franks in the North, "there are believers and preachers of the Gospel confessing the resurrection from the dead; and so we see the prophecies being fulfilled over the whole world."[9] Meanwhile, at home, there were signs of the end. In 542, the first recorded outbreak of bubonic plague in Europe halved the population of Constantinople. In 557, a major earthquake brought down the dome of Hagia Sophia, and many people believed that the end of the world was at hand.[10]

The world, of course, did not end. Hagia Sophia's dome was rebuilt with a stronger

---

7. Cyril Mango, *Byzantium: The Empire of New Rome* (London: Weidenfeld & Nicolson, 1980), p. 1.
8. Maximus the Confessor, *The Church's Mystagogy,* trans. George C. Berthold, in *Maximus Confessor: Selected Writings,* Classics of Western Spirituality (Mahwah, N.J.: Paulist Press, 1985).
9. Quoted in Mango, *Byzantium,* pp. 185-86.
10. Mango, *Byzantium,* pp. 204-5.

A Tenth-Century Mosaic from Hagia Sophia. In this particular mosaic, Mary, holding the Christ child, is flanked by emperors Justinian (left) and Constantine (right). See p. 30 for details.

Source: Art Resource, NY

design. The western territories regained by Justinian were lost again in subsequent centuries. Hopes for the quick completion of world evangelization were dashed by the rise of Islam and the Arab conquests of the seventh century, which cost the empire its eastern and southern provinces. "The catastrophic reverse that Christianity suffered . . . was totally unexpected," writes Cyril Mango, "and it may be said that Byzantine thinking never adjusted to it."[11] The Byzantines always seemed to display an optimism that was belied by their circumstances. Even when the limits of their own empire were shrinking before advancing Arab, Slav, Western Christian, and Turkish armies, and even after the final fall of Constantinople in 1453, Byzantine Christians retained a strong sense of the imminence of God's Kingdom. Their confidence was rooted in their faith and was due in no small part to the liturgy. It is in the liturgy, the gathering of the Christian community for worship, that the Kingdom of God is most clearly manifested.

The worship in Constantinople filled time and space. Every morning and evening was marked by popular sung **matins** and **vespers** (services consisting mainly of psalms and prayers). Lengthy nighttime **vigils** of hymn-singing and Scripture reading, sometimes lasting throughout the night, prepared worshipers to celebrate the Lord's Supper on Saturdays, Sundays, and feast days. It is likely that the sixth-century deacon and hymnographer Romanos the Melodist composed his *kontakia* — sung sermons of twenty-four stanzas with refrains for popular participation — for these vigils. (See pp. 105-12 and pp. 113-20.) On **stational days**, special occasions, elaborate processions of clergy and laity, often including the emperor and the imperial court, wound through the streets from church to church with psalm- and hymn-singing. This turned the whole city into a place of worship and reminded the people that they were all one church. But the central act of worship was the Divine "**Synaxis**," the "assembly" or "gathering together" — that is, the communion service or **Eucharist**. The Synaxis took the worshipers beyond time and space through two complementary movements: convergence

Stational days are days on which is prescribed a liturgical procession from one church to another, culminating with the celebration of the Eucharist.

Synaxis comes from the verb *synagein,* meaning "to bring or gather together." The word *synagogue* comes from the same verb.

11. Mango, *Byzantium,* p. 186.

and ascent, movement toward union with one another in Christ and movement toward heaven. Both movements culminate in the Kingdom of God.

The movement of "gathering together" began in the worshipers' homes as they set out to go to church. On stational days, when the Eucharist was prescribed for a particular church, it might include a gathering for prayer in one of the cities' forums and a procession to the church of the day. As the worshipers approached the church, they would stop to leave their gifts of bread and wine at the **skeuophylakion**, a building just outside of the church where such gifts were collected. (Some of these gifts would be used for communion; the rest would be distributed to the poor.) Arriving at the church, they would gather in the open atrium at the west end or in one of the courtyards on the sides to wait for the patriarch (as the bishop of Constantinople was called). The patriarch entered the church before the people, preceded by a deacon carrying the **Book of the Gospels,** a decoratively bound book containing the Four Gospels. When the patriarch had passed through the central western, "Imperial" or "Royal" doors of the nave, the people would pour in from all sides. (For this entrance Hagia Sophia had nine doors at the western end of the nave, four each on the north and south sides, and two on the eastern end, one on each side of the apse.) The patriarch made his way down the solea, venerated the altar, and then went up to his throne, where he turned to bless the people. Then began the reading of Scripture.[12]

The movement toward union did not end with this entrance into the church but continued in the liturgy with the **kiss of peace.** This was a real kiss on the mouth — although in the sixth century, it was given only by men to men and women to women. It was understood to be a sharing in the Spirit (*pneuma,* a Greek word which means both "breath" and "spirit") and was reserved for the baptized faithful.[13] Right after the Bible readings and the sermon, and right before the kiss, the non-baptized catechumens were dismissed, and the doors of the church were closed. The kiss was followed by the Nicene-Constantinopolitan **Creed** recited in unison to show the worshipers were united in faith. The movement of convergence culminated in communion of "the holy things for the holy people" (the early call to communion). Here the communicants realized their union with "the one holy one, the one Lord Jesus Christ, to the glory of God the Father" (the response to the call to communion), and with each other in fulfillment of the Eucharistic prayer, which had asked that "all of us who partake of the one bread and the cup" may be "unite[d] with one another . . . into the fellowship of the Holy Spirit" (Anaphora of St. Basil). The ultimate goal of communion as well as of the entire prayer of the community was to be able "with one mouth and one heart to glorify [God's] all-honorable and magnificent name, Father, Son, and Holy Spirit, now and ever, and unto ages of ages" (from the concluding doxology of the Eucharistic anaphora).

---

12. For the order of worship and the liturgical texts cited in the following paragraphs, consult the section "Order of Service and Texts," pp. 83-103.

13. See L. Edward Phillips, *The Ritual Kiss in Early Christian Worship* (Cambridge: Grove Books, 1996).

It was the practice in early Christianity that what was offered in the worship service came from the congregation's offerings for the general use of the church. Usually these offerings were "in kind"—that is, bread, wine, church implements, and so on. The offerings were presented in different ways in different places.

The central passage into the nave from the west was called the "Imperial" or "Royal" doors because the emperor passed through them.

The dismissal of the **catechumens** was a significant transition in both the order of service and the make-up of the congregation. The catechumens, those studying for baptism, could attend only the first part of the service, often called the **Liturgy of the Catechumens,** which centered on Bible readings and sermon. Only the already baptized could attend the second part, called the **Liturgy of the Faithful,** which consisted of prayers and communion.

A creed is a statement of faith agreed to by a church council. The Byzantine church used the creed formulated at the general councils of Nicea and Constantinople in the fourth century.

The Eucharist was also understood as an ascent to heaven. It was the "bloodless sacrifice," as Paul the Silentiary called it in his description of Hagia Sophia (p. 75). He was no doubt quoting the Byzantine Anaphora of St. John Chrysostom, but it was a common term for the Eucharist in other early Christian Eucharistic prayers as well. In early Jewish-Christian tradition, as evidenced by the second-century **Testament of Levi**, the bloodless sacrifice was that which the highest ranks of angels offered God in the highest heaven "for all the sins of ignorance of the righteous."[14] By participating in this bloodless worship, the early Christians understood themselves to be participating in the angelic worship.

At least since Isidore of Seville (a scholarly archbishop in Spain) defined the Greek word *Eucharist* for Latin speakers as "good gift" (from the Greek: *eu* = "good," *charis* = "gift") in the early seventh century,[15] Western Christianity has (until recently) tended to see the Eucharist almost exclusively as a gift coming from God to humans. The Christian East, on the other hand, has always understood the Eucharist according to its original Greek sense — as thanksgiving offered to God. It is first Christ's thank offering, and this thank offering is Christ himself in the human nature he brings to the Father, in which we also participate. The gift God gives is the ability to participate in Christ's offering through liturgy. The Anaphora of John Chrysostom concludes its opening praise by giving thanks "for this liturgy" and asking that God "vouchsafe[16] to receive it at our hands, even though there stand before you thousands of archangels and hosts of angels, the cherubim and the seraphim . . . singing the triumphal hymn . . . : 'Holy, Holy, Holy.'"

From the beginning of the Synaxis the people were aware that they were participating in heavenly worship. As the patriarch entered the church, he would stop to pray that "the holy angels may enter with us, to serve and glorify your goodness with us." As the people entered, following the bishop, they would sing a refrain based on the hymn of the angels from Isaiah 6:3, "Holy God, Holy Mighty, Holy Immortal, have mercy on us," while a soloist sang the first six verses of Psalm 95: "Come, let us sing for joy to the LORD; let us shout aloud to the Rock of our salvation. Let us come before him with thanksgiving and extol him with music and song. . . ." The image of heavenly ascent was presented in the person of the patriarch as he continued his procession into the sanctuary and climbed up to his throne at the top of the synthronon.

Images of heavenly worship intensified during the Liturgy of the Faithful, after the catechumens had been dismissed and the doors shut, separating the faithful baptized from life in this world. After the intercessory prayer of the faithful, deacons would bring bread and wine for the Eucharist in a procession from the skeuophylakion to the altar. During this

Processions in Byzantine worship gave the worshipers a sense of movement from city to church, from nave to sanctuary, and from earth to heaven. A particularly important one happened after the catechumens were dismissed: deacons went out to the skeuophylakion, a small building to the north of the church, to get some of the bread and wine left by people on their way to church. The deacons brought these back through the center of the nave, around the ambo, and to the altar table to be used for communion. This procession grew to be elaborate, involving not only clergy but also the emperor.

14. Testament of Levi 3.5, translated by H. C. Kee, "Testaments of the Twelve Patriarchs," in J. H. Charlesworth, *The Old Testament Pseudepigrapha I: Apocalyptic Literature and Testaments* (Garden City, N.Y.: Doubleday, 1983), p. 789.

15. Isidore of Seville, *Etymologies,* VI.19.39.

16. "Vouchsafe" is a command in the earliest manuscript of Chrysostom's anaphora, the translation of which is furnished in this book (see pp. 93-99). In other versions it is part of a relative clause qualifying "liturgy": "We thank you for this liturgy, which you vouchsafe to receive at our hands."

Mysteries is an east-
ern Christian term for
sacraments in general
and the Eucharistic
gifts in particular.

"Entry of the **Mysteries**," a soloist would intone verses from Psalm 24 about the entrance of the King of glory into the sanctuary (Ps. 24:7-10) while the faithful would respond with allelu-ias, which is also a heavenly hymn (cf. Rev. 19:1-8). In 573 the refrain verse was expanded to make the imagery more explicit. In this "**Cherubic Hymn**" the faithful were said to "mysti-cally represent [literally, "be the icon of"] the cherubim and sing the thrice-holy hymn to the life-giving Trinity" and were called upon to "lay aside all earthly cares" in order to "receive the King of all, invisibly escorted by the angelic orders." The movement of ascent reached its apex in the Eucharistic prayer when the faithful raised their hearts "on high . . . with the Lord" (from the opening dialog of the Eucharistic anaphora). There they joined the eternal thanksgiving, singing "Holy, Holy, Holy" with the angels and entering into communion with the King of all.

The liturgy's inherent symbolism of convergence and ascent is captured neatly by the sev-enth-century monk Maximus the Confessor in *The Church's Msytagogy,* the earliest witness to the developed Byzantine liturgy (see pp. 49-64).[17] Using marriage as the image of union, Maximus sees the closing of the doors after the dismissal of the catechumens as a symbol of the entrance of the worthy into the nuptial chamber of Christ (*Myst.* 15). The kiss of peace before the creed symbolizes "the concord, unanimity, and identity of views which we shall all have among ourselves in faith and love at the time of the revelation of the ineffable blessings to come" as well as "intimate familiarity with the Word of God" (*Myst.* 17). The "Holy, Holy, Holy" during the Eucharistic prayer, he says, "represents the union and the equality of honor to be manifested in the future with the incorporeal and intelligent powers" — that is, the an-gels (*Myst.* 19). The Lord's Prayer, the prayer in which we pray to God as "our Father," shows adoption through the gift of the Holy Spirit "once every human particularity is overcome" (*Myst.* 20). "The profession 'One is Holy' and what follows," Maximus continues, "represent the gathering and union beyond reason and understanding which will take place between those who have been mystically and wisely initiated by God and the mysterious oneness of the divine simplicity in the incorruptible age of the spiritual world" (*Myst.* 21). Finally, "the distribution of the mysteries" (communion) shows those who receive it worthily "that they . . . can be . . . gods by adoption through grace because all of God entirely fills them and leaves no part of them empty of his presence" (*Myst.* 21). The movements of convergence and assent thus lead to the union with God that Byzantine writers call *theosis,* **deification** or **divinization**, which is how Byzantine theology understands salvation.

For Eastern Chris-
tianity, *theosis* is
the converse and
consequence of the
Incarnation. A divine
person, the Son of
God, took on human
nature so that human
persons might share
in divine nature. The
sharing comes about
through union with
God in Christ.

Justinian's Church of Hagia Sophia and the Byzantine liturgy were made for each other. The church and its furnishings were designed to accommodate the liturgy's processions and draw out its inherent symbolism of convergence and ascent. The liturgy, in turn, adapted itself to the spaces of Hagia Sophia. The entrances and exits became more elaborate; new

17. Maximus the Confessor, *The Church's Mystagogy,* in *Maximus Confessor: Selected Writings,* pp. 181-225. Subsequent references to this volume will be made parenthetically in the text.

hymns, such as the Cherubic Hymn at the entrance of the Eucharistic gifts, and prayers, such as the Prayer behind the Ambo after the dismissal, were added to accompany them.

Today's Byzantine liturgy retains many of the features of the liturgy of Hagia Sophia, though they are somewhat obscured by the need to adapt them to smaller spaces. The liturgy presents an image of the fullness of future salvation, the Kingdom of God. Through the liturgy, the future Kingdom is experienced now. In liturgy the worshipers experience "the unity of the Spirit in the bond of peace" in the one body of Christ (Eph. 4:3ff.). They realize in themselves that God has "made us alive together with Christ . . . and raised us up with him and seated us with him in the heavenly places in Christ Jesus" (Eph. 2:4-6). They have a taste of heaven on earth.

Documenting the Community's Worship

People and Artifacts

Sixth-Century Liturgical Vessels

The silver communion **chalice** (the cup, to hold and distribute the wine) and **paten** (the plate for the Eucharistic bread) were possibly made in Constantinople for a rural church in Syria. The chalice bears the stamp of the emperor Justinian (527-565) and the paten that of Justin II (565-578). Around the rim of the chalice, which measures 6 ½ inches in diameter, is inscribed the offering formula from the Anaphora of Basil: "Your own of your own we offer unto you, O Lord." The paten measures nearly 14 inches in diameter. A scene called the Communion of the Apostles shows Christ twice: on the right he gives the apostles the communion bread; on the left, the communion wine. On the altar table, which is draped with an altar cloth, are a chalice, two wineskins, and a paten. At the bottom of the image are two more liturgical vessels, a pitcher and a basin used for washing the patriarch's hands before the anaphora. Columns topped by a beam called an **architrave** define the liturgical space around the altar table. The inscription shows that this paten was donated "for the repose (of the soul) of Sergia, daughter of John, and of Theodosius, and for the salvation of Megalos and Nonnous and their children." Such "votive" donations were a type of prayer.

Source: "Riha" Paten and Chalice, 6th century, Constantinople or Syria. Images copyright Dumbarton Oaks, Byzantine Collection, Washington, D.C.

A Tenth-Century Mosaic from Hagia Sophia

In this particular mosaic, emperors Justinian (left) and Constantine (right) present, respectively, the church of Hagia Sophia and the city of Constantinople to Christ enthroned on Mary's lap.

Source: Erich Lessing/Art Resource, NY

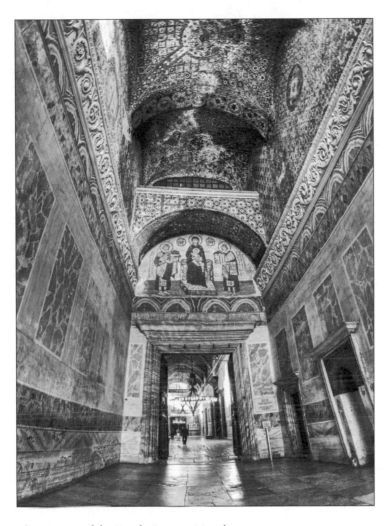

The Context of the Tenth-Century Mosaic

The mosaic featuring Mary, Justinian, and Constantine is found above an inner door on the southwest porch of Hagia Sophia.

Source: Hans Mast

Mosaics Portraying the Initial Entrance Procession

In these two complementary mosaic panels from the sanctuary area of a sixth-century Byzantine church in Ravenna, Italy, the imperial couple, Justinian I and Theodora, their attendants, and clergy are represented as entering a church for worship.

In the first panel, the emperor is led by the local bishop, Maximianus. To the right of the bishop, a deacon carries the Gospel book, bound in gold and set with pearls and emeralds. Another carries incense. In the second panel, the empress is preceded by deacons and accompanied by ladies of the court. Both emperor and empress bring gifts for the church: the emperor carries a paten or bowl (for the Eucharistic bread) and the empress carrries a chalice (for the Eucharistic wine).

Neither Justinian nor Theodora ever visited Ravenna, but modern scholars believe that these are accurate representations made from portraits brought there after the city was recaptured in 540.

Source (for both mosaic panels): Cameraphoto Arte, Venice/Art Resource, NY

A Sixth-Century Icon of Christ Possibly Dedicated by Emperor Justinian I

Icons were perhaps originally created or commissioned as acts of thanksgiving for prayers answered and used for personal devotion. This icon of Christ, from the St. Catherine's Monastery on Sinai, may have been donated by Justinian when he founded the monastery in the early sixth century.[1] By the sixth century, if not earlier, icons were found in churches, giving them a role in public worship. In this icon, Christ has the same pose as in the image sewn in silk on the front of the altar cloth of Hagia Sophia as described by Paul the Silentiary:[2] "He seems to be stretching out the fingers of the right hand, as if preaching His immortal words, while in His left He holds the book of divine message — the book that tells what He, the Lord, accomplished with provident mind when His foot trod the earth."[3] The people would have seen their own ministers assume this pose and so would have had the sense that Christ himself was presiding over their worship.

Source: The Blessing Christ, first half of the sixth century, from the Holy Monastery of Saint Catherine, Sinai, Egypt. Photo credit: Jim Forest

1. See Thomas F. Mathews, "Early Icons of the Holy Monastery of Saint Catherine at Sinai," in *Holy Image, Hallowed Ground: Icons from Sinai,* ed. Robert S. Nelson and Kristen M. Collins (Los Angeles: J. Paul Getty Museum, 2006), pp. 51-52.

2. To see this quotation in context, refer to p. 76.

3. Translated by Cyril Mango in *The Art of the Byzantine Empire, 312-1453: Sources and Documents* (Englewood Cliffs, N.J.: Prentice Hall, 1972), p. 89.

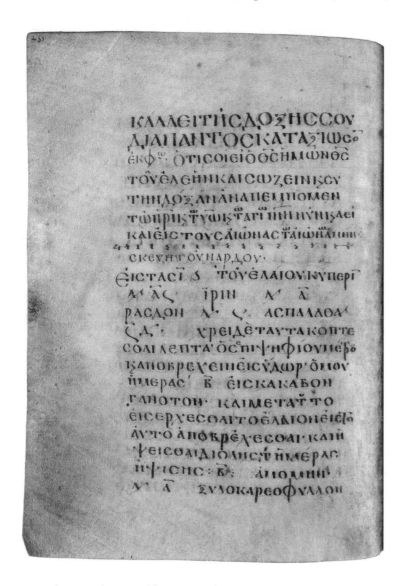

An Early Byzantine Worship Manuscript

This is a page from the oldest surviving Byzantine prayer book, known by its shelf number in the Vatican's Barberini Library as Barberini Greek 336. The manuscript dates from the mid- to late eighth century and comes from southern Italy, a region that was part of the Byzantine empire into the eleventh century. It contains the presider's prayers for the liturgies of Basil and John Chrysostom as well as some other services. Although the order of service has changed somewhat from the sixth century, many of the prayers are likely the same. In Constantinople's worship, Scripture would have been read from books like this one, but prayers were likely read from scrolls like the one pictured in Basil's hands in the fresco on p. 36.

Source: © Biblioteca Apostolica Vaticana; used by permission

A Fresco Showing the Use of a Prayer Scroll at Worship

Although Basil the Great was never bishop of Constantinople, the liturgy bearing his name was the principal Sunday order of service there in the sixth century. In this eleventh- or twelfth-century fresco from Hagia Sophia (named for the cathedral in Constantinople) in Ohrid, Macedonia, Basil is shown at the altar table reading a prayer from his liturgy, written on a scroll. (In Constantinople, books were used for Scripture, while scrolls were used for liturgical texts.) The liturgical furnishings in the fresco are Byzantine, with a ciborium over the altar table. Basil has bowed his head for prayer after the Byzantine fashion.

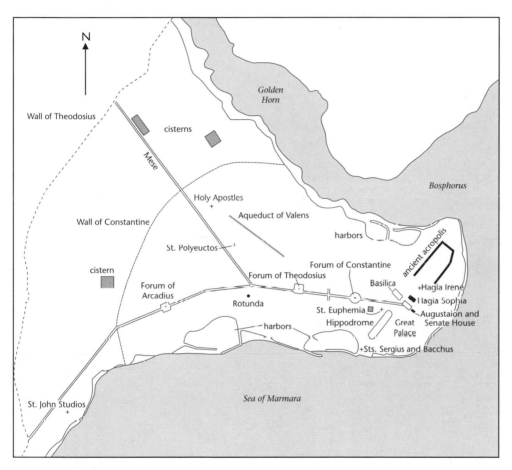

A Plan of Early Constantinople

This map shows the principal churches in the city. Hagia Sophia is toward the tip of the peninsula on the northeast side of the square known as the **Augustaion,** the seat of government of the Roman Empire. Opposite Hagia Sophia were the royal palace and the **hippodrome,** where the masses met both to watch the chariot races and to acclaim a new emperor. The Senate house was located on the southeastern side of the square. On the corner of the square was mile-marker one, from which all distances in the empire were measured.

Source: Rowland J. Mainstone, *Hagia Sophia: Architecture, Structure, and Liturgy of Justinian's Great Church* (New York: Thames and Hudson, 1988), image 157 on p. 133.

Hagia Sophia, Interior

This 1852 lithograph by Louis Haghe captures the church's immensity. None of the furnishings depicted are original; they date from the Turkish period (1453 to present).

Source: Bildarchiv Preussicher Kulturbesitz/Art Resource, NY

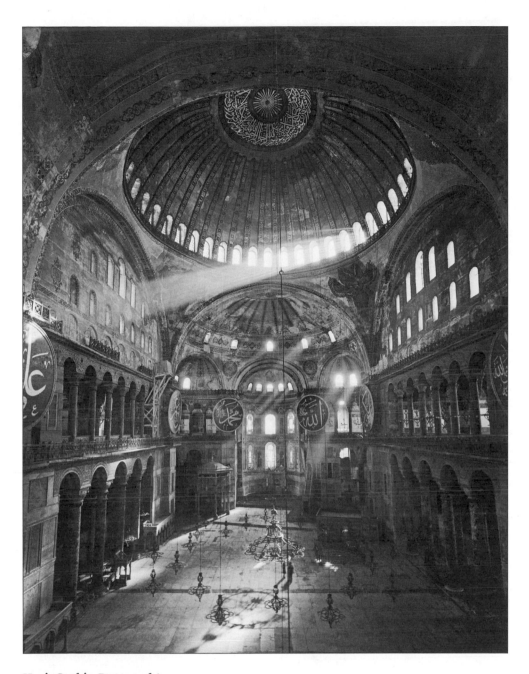

Hagia Sophia, Dome and Apse

Morning light streams in through the windows around the dome and in the eastern apse of the church, giving a sense of what worshipers at the Sunday-morning Eucharist must have experienced. Hagia Sophia was designed to make maximum use of sunlight.

Source: Erich Lessing/Art Resource, NY

Hagia Sophia from the South

The following images show the building in its modern state from the south. The tall towers, or minarets, were added during the Turkish period, when the building was used as a mosque. (Today it is a museum.) To lead worship, the bishop would have entered from the west (the left side of the building as pictured) and processed to the east (the right side). The first image shows Hagia Sophia from eye level, while the second shows it from a higher elevation. According to Procopius, the sixth-century historian (see p. 66), the building "soars to a height to match the sky, and as if surging up from amongst the other buildings it stands on high and looks down upon the remainder of the city. . . ."

Source: Art Resource, NY

Source: Rowland J. Mainstone, *Hagia Sophia: The Architecture, Structure, and Liturgy of Justinian's Great Church* (New York: Thames & Hudson, 1988), image 15 on page 23.

A Cutaway View of Hagia Sophia from the North

This artist's rendering of Hagia Sophia with worshipers present gives a sense of the complexity of the church's design and the vast space the structure enclosed. (Reconstruction of structures and furnishings on the facing page is to some extent conjectural.)

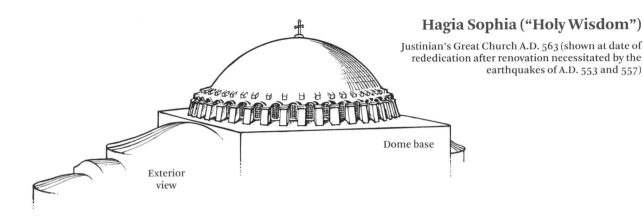

Hagia Sophia ("Holy Wisdom")

Justinian's Great Church A.D. 563 (shown at date of rededication after renovation necessitated by the earthquakes of A.D. 553 and 557)

Dome base

Exterior view

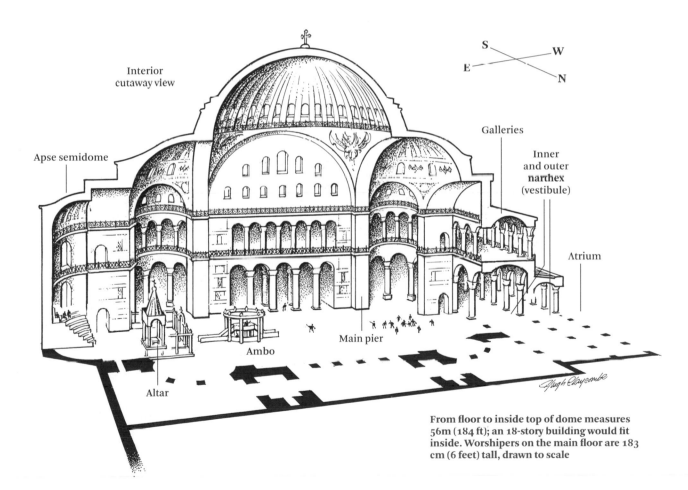

Interior cutaway view

Galleries

Inner and outer **narthex** (vestibule)

Apse semidome

Atrium

Main pier

Ambo

Altar

From floor to inside top of dome measures 56m (184 ft); an 18-story building would fit inside. Worshipers on the main floor are 183 cm (6 feet) tall, drawn to scale

A Possible Arrangement of the Principal Furnishings at the Time of the Second Dedication
This artist's rendering of the eastern end of Hagia Sophia based on eyewitness accounts shows the centers where major liturgical activities would have taken place. The ambo was for Scripture readings. The altar table with the ciborium was the site for consecrating the bread and wine for communion. The synthronon held the bishop's chair, which was surrounded by places for other clergy. (Reconstruction of structures and furnishings on the facing page is to some extent conjectural.)

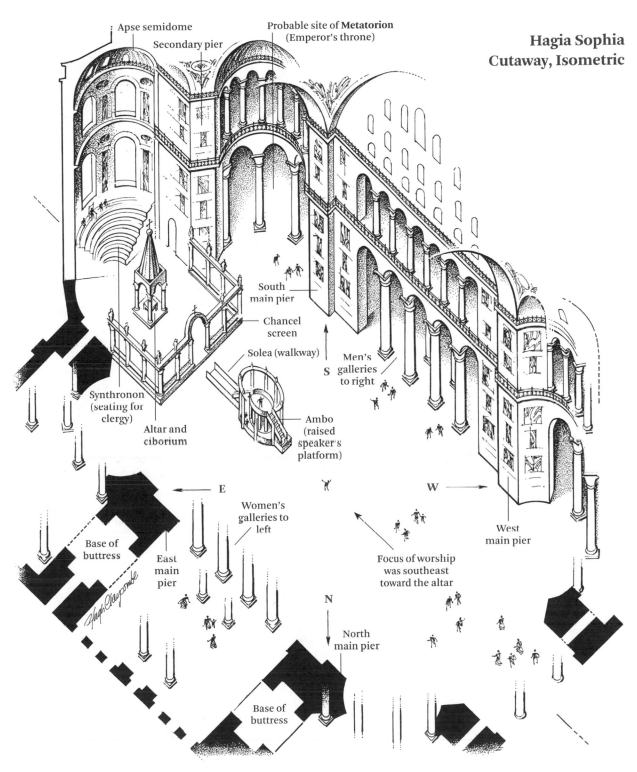

Apse semidome

Secondary pier

Probable site of **Metatorion**
(Emperor's throne)

Hagia Sophia
Cutaway, Isometric

South
main pier

Chancel
screen

Solea (walkway)

S

Men's
galleries
to right

Synthronon
(seating for
clergy)

Altar and
ciborium

Ambo
(raised
speaker's
platform)

E

Women's
galleries to
left

W

West
main pier

Base of
buttress

East
main
pier

Focus of worship
was southeast
toward the altar

N

North
main pier

Base of
buttress

© Hugh Claycombe 2011

Hagia Sophia from the East

Approaching the church by sea from the east, one can see how it dominates the eastern end of the peninsula. Procopius says, "The whole city is viewed from there as from a watchtower." The half-domes in front of and descending from the main dome like steps covered the altar area and the apse, which contained the synthronon, the elevated seats of the patriarch and other clergy.

Source: Hans Mast

A View of the Nave from the West

This is the view from the gallery (balcony) over the inner narthex looking east toward the altar area and clergy space. None of the original furnishings are present. From this perspective, the sixth-century worshiper would have seen the ambo in the center of the nave and, beyond it, the ciborium over the altar table. Directly below this gallery are the Royal or **Imperial doors**, entranceway of the emperor (see p. 48). The beauty and vastness of the space reinforced the notion of entering into the heavenly realm to worship.

In the sixth century, people were astonished by the central dome of Hagia Sophia. According to Paul the Silentiary, the massive dome seemed to float; it was "like the firmament which rests on air (see p. 72)."

Source: Interior of the Hagia Sophia seen from the gallery reserved for the Empress and her entourage, sixth century. Photo credit: Werner Forman/Art Resource, NY

A View of the Nave Looking toward the Royal or Imperial Doors

This is the view looking west from the nave toward the Imperial or Royal doors. The patriarch and, on certain days, the emperor entered through this central doorway while worshipers poured in from other doors surrounding the building to begin the Eucharistic liturgy.

Source: Hans Mast

Descriptions of Worship

A Description of the Order of Worship and Its Meaning

The following excerpts come from a document entitled Mystagogia, *written by a monk named Maximus the Confessor in the early seventh century. Maximus earned his title "the Confessor" by being tortured for his rejection of "Monotheletism," the idea that Christ had only one will, the will he had as a member of the Trinity, an idea first put forward by the emperor Heraclius in an effort to reconcile non-Chalcedonians (see "The Context of the Worshiping Community" and "Timeline"). Maximus died in exile in 662 but was vindicated by the Council of Constantinople of 680, which said that Christ had both a divine will and a human will.*

The title given to this work refers as much to the genre as to the work itself. "Mystagogy" means initiation into mysteries. Paul spoke of the "mystery hidden throughout all ages and generations," which God had made known through Christ; it was, in fact, Christ himself (Col. 1:26-27, 2:2-3). The mystery was the revelation in Christ of God's "plan for the fullness of time" (Eph. 1:9-10). The early Christians called the bread and wine of communion, the whole Lord's Supper service, and eventually other acts of worship "mysteries," a practice that continued among the Greek-, Syriac-, and Slavic-speaking Christians. In the fourth century, there arose the practice of mystagogical preaching, in which the services of baptism and the Lord's Supper were explained to the newly baptized so they could understand what they had just experienced. Maximus takes this one step further, writing a mystagogical treatise for mature Christians. His is the first in a long line of commentaries on the order of worship that continues among Byzantine-rite Christians into the present day (see Alexander Schmemann's The Eucharist*). These vary in their approach according to the times in which they were written. But they all seek to show the meaning of worship with respect to God's plan for the fullness of time.*

Probably written for the instruction of fellow monks, Maximus's Mystagogia *offers details about early Byzantine worship. Since no manuscript of liturgical texts or instructions remains from this early period, this writing is an especially important witness to this way of worship.[1] Viewing the liturgy as a means of spiritual ascent to union with God through Christ, Maximus walks through many of the main features of a Eucharistic service from start to finish, interpreting them in this light. (The reader may wish to follow Maximus through the service using the reconstructed order; see pp. 83-92.)*

---

1. On the Byzantine character of Maximus's liturgy, in response to a recent suggestion to the contrary, see Robert F. Taft, "Is the Liturgy Described in the Mystagogia of Maximus Confessor Byzantine, Palestinian or Neither?" *Bollettino della Badia Greca di Grottaferrata* 3rd series 8 (2011): 223-70.

Introduction

The "blessed old man" may be a real person (e.g., Maximus's teacher) or a literary device Maximus uses to shift credit for his ideas away from himself out of a sense of modesty. (For the possibilities, see Berthold, *Maximus Confessor,* p. 215, n. 4.)

. . . For you heard me once relate, in a brief and cursory way, the beautiful and mystical reflections of a certain grand old man and truly wise in divine matters, about the holy Church and the holy synaxis performed in it. And as they are especially rich in teaching value, you hastened to ask me to make a written account of these things for you, wanting to have my writing as a remedy against forgetfulness and as an aid for the memory. . . .

But I do not promise to narrate in order everything that the blessed old man mystically contemplated, nor will these words proceed from his contemplation and elaboration of them. For this man, because he was truly wise and a teacher in all learning, had rendered himself free from the bonds of matter and its fantasies by the abundance of virtue and very long and knowing familiarity in divine realities and by his laborious industry, and so really possessed a mind illuminated by divine light and could thus see what others do not see. In addition, he had the gift of words to explain most accurately the object of his contemplations, and like a mirror which is not obscured by any stain of the passions, he had the power of both understanding and speaking about things which others could not perceive, so that those who listened to him could be brought to see the whole meaning of his discourse, the whole content of his thoughts clearly perceived in all their meaning and transferred to them through the medium of his words. But such things I remember and can comprehend dimly and speak of even more dimly, but devoutly and with the grace of God who illumines obscure things. . . .

In the introduction to his work, Maximus sets out a foundational principle of Byzantine theology, which is also the primary problem confronting the human creature: God is by nature unknowable and unapproachable for humans. In the remainder of the work, Maximus shows how this unbridgeable distance between Creator and creatures is overcome in the worship of the church and in life.

But let God be the guide of our words and our concepts, the sole intelligence of intelligent beings and intelligible things, the meaning behind those who speak and of what is spoken, the life of those who live and those who receive life, who is and who becomes all for all beings, through whom everything is and becomes but who by himself never is nor becomes in any way anything that ever is or becomes in any manner. In this way he can in no way be associated by nature with any being, and thus because of his superbeing is more fittingly referred to as nonbeing. For since it is necessary that we understand correctly the difference between God and creatures, then the affirmation of superbeing must be the negation of beings, and the affirmation of beings must be the negation of superbeing. In fact, both names, being and nonbeing, are to be reverently applied to him, although not at all properly. In one sense they are both proper to him, one affirming the being of God as cause of beings, the other completely denying in him the being which all beings have, based on his pre-eminence as cause. On the other hand, neither is proper to him because neither represents in any way an affirmation of the essence of the being under discussion as to its substance or nature. For nothing whatsoever, whether being or nonbeing, is linked to him as a cause, no being or what is called being, no nonbeing, or what is called nonbeing, is properly close to him. He has in fact a simple existence, unknowable and inaccessible to all and altogether beyond understanding which transcends all affirmation and negation. But so much for this; let us come to the subject we propose to treat.

Chapter One

How and in what manner holy Church is an image and figure of God.

Now that blessed old man used to say that at the first level of contemplation holy Church bears the imprint and image of God, since it has the same activity as he does by imitation and in figure. For God, who made and brought into existence all things by his infinite power, contains, gathers, and limits them, and in his Providence binds both intelligible and sensible beings to himself and to one another. Maintaining about himself as cause, beginning, and end of all beings which are by nature distant from one another, he makes them converge in each other by the singular force of their relationship to him as origin. Through this force he leads all beings to a common and unconfused identity of movement and existence, no one being originally in revolt against any other or separated from him by a difference of nature or of movement, but all things combine with all others in an unconfused way by the singular indissoluble relation to and protection of the one principle and cause. This reality abolishes and dims all their particular relations considered according to each one's nature, but not by dissolving or destroying them or putting an end to their existence. Rather, it does so by transcending them and revealing them, as the whole reveals its parts or as the whole is revealed in its cause by which the same whole and its parts came into being and appearance, since they have their whole cause surpassing them in splendor. And just as the sun outshines the stars both in nature and in energy, so also does it conceal their existence from those who look for their cause. For just as the parts come from the whole, so do effects properly proceed and get known from the cause and hold their particularities still when understood with exclusive reference to the cause and, as was said, according to the singular force of their relationship to it. For being all in all, the God who transcends all in infinite measure will be seen only by those who are pure in understanding when the mind in contemplative recollection of the principles of beings will end up with God as cause, principle, and end of all, the creation and beginning of all things and eternal ground of the circuit of things.

It is in this way that the holy Church of God will be shown to be working for us the same effects as God, in the same way as the image reflects its archetype. For numerous and of almost infinite number are the men, women, and children who are distinct from one another and vastly different by birth and appearance, by nationality and language, by customs and age, by opinions and skills, by manners and habits, by pursuits and studies, and still again by reputation, fortune, characteristics, and connections: All are born into the Church and through it are reborn and recreated in the Spirit. To all in equal measure it gives and bestows one divine form and designation, to be Christ's and to carry his name. In accordance with

Maximus uses the terms *image, imprint* or *type,* and *symbol* interchangeably. The image connects levels or orders of being. An archetype on a higher level appears on a lower level as its image. Image and archetype are not static, but are alike in their activities. God holds all things together on the cosmic level by relationship to himself. Likewise, the church as the assembly of believers holds all its members in unity by their common relationship to Christ. Maximus's ideas contributed to the Byzantine theology of icons (image = Greek *eikon*).

The beginning of the solution to the problem that Maximus posed in the introduction — that God is unknowable and unapproachable — is to recognize that God is the Creator and therefore has a relationship with creatures as their "cause, principle, and end."

faith it gives to all a single, simple, whole and indivisible condition which does not allow us to bring to mind the existence of the myriads of differences among them, even if they do exist, through the universal relationship and union of all things with it. It is through it that absolutely no one at all is in himself separated from the community, since everyone converges with all the rest and joins together with them by the one, simple, and indivisible grace and power of faith. "For all," it is said, "had but one heart and one mind" [Acts 4:32]. Thus to be and to appear as one body formed of different members is really worthy of Christ himself, our true head, in whom, says the divine Apostle, "there is neither male nor female, neither Jew nor Greek, neither circumcision nor uncircumcision, neither foreigner nor Scythian, neither slave nor freeman, but Christ is everything in all of you."[2] It is he who encloses in himself all beings by the unique, simple, and infinitely wise power of his goodness. As the center of straight lines that radiate from him, he does not allow by his unique, simple, and single cause and power that the principles of beings become disjoined at the periphery, but rather he circumscribes their extension in a circle and brings back to himself the distinctive elements of beings which he himself brought into existence. The purpose of this is so that the creations and products of the one God be in no way strangers and enemies to one another by having no reason or center for which they might show each other any friendly or peaceful sentiment or identity, and not run the risk of having their being separated from God to dissolve into nonbeing.

Thus, as has been said, the holy Church of God is an image of God because it realizes the same union of the faithful with God. As different as they are by language, places, and customs, they are made one by it through faith. God realizes this union among the natures of things without confusing them but in lessening and bringing together their distinction, as was shown, in a relationship and union with himself as cause, principle, and end.

Chapter Two
Why, how, and in what manner the holy Church of God is an image of the world composed of visible and invisible substances.

On a second level of contemplation, he used to speak of God's holy Church as a figure and image of the entire world composed of visible and invisible essences because, like it, it contains both unity and diversity.

For while it is one house in its construction, it admits of a certain diversity in the disposition of its plan by being divided into an area exclusively assigned to priests and ministers, which we call a sanctuary, and one accessible to all the faithful, which we call a nave. [See the division in Hagia Sophia on p. 45.] Still, it is one in its basic reality without being divided into its parts by reason of the differences between them; but rather by their relationship to the

---

Sidebar (left column):

For Maximus, unity in the church does not negate the uniqueness of each of its members. Maximus speaks of this unity in the same terms that Byzantine theology uses to speak about both the relationship of the Three Persons of the Trinity and the two natures in Christ. It is the language of the Council of Chalcedon, which affirmed that Christ's human and divine natures are in union "without confusion" (see p. 4). We find this "Incarnational principle" throughout the treatise.

Maximus continues his discussion of unity in diversity by using the church building as an example. The divisions in the building reflect the different roles of clergy and laity in the order of worship. The parts, while distinct, form a unity. Each exists for the sake of the other and in relationship to the whole (building or worship service).

---

2. Maximus combines Galatians 3:28 and Colossians 3:10. When Byzantine writers refer to *the* Apostle, they mean Paul.

unity it frees these parts from the difference arising from their names. It shows to each other that they are both the same thing, and reveals that one is to the other in turn what each one is for itself. Thus, the nave is the sanctuary in potency by being consecrated by the relationship of the sacrament toward its end, and in turn the sanctuary is the nave in act by possessing the principle of its own sacrament, which remains one and the same in its two parts. In this way the entire world of beings produced by God in creation is divided into a spiritual world filled with intelligible and incorporeal essences and into this sensible and bodily world which is ingeniously woven together of many forms and natures. This is like another sort of Church not of human construction which is wisely revealed in this church which is humanly made, and it has for its sanctuary the higher world assigned to the powers above, and for its nave the lower world, which is reserved [for] those who share the life of sense.

Once again, there is but one world, and it is not divided by its parts. On the contrary, it encloses the differences of the parts arising from their natural properties by their relationship to what is one and indivisible in itself. Moreover, it shows that both are the same thing with it and alternately with each other in an unconfused way and that the whole of one enters into the whole of the other, and both fill the same whole as parts fill a unit, and in this way the parts are uniformly and entirely filled as a whole. For the whole spiritual world seems mystically imprinted on the whole sensible world in symbolic forms, for those who are capable of seeing this, and conversely the whole sensible world is spiritually explained in the mind in the principles which it contains. In the spiritual world it is in principles; in the sensible world it is in figures. And their function was like a wheel within a wheel,[3] as says the marvelous seer of extraordinary things, Ezekiel, in speaking, I think, of the two worlds. And again, "The invisible realities from the creation of the world have been perceived and are recognized through the things he has made," says the divine Apostle [Rom. 1:20]. And if we perceive what does not appear by means of what does, as the Scripture has it, then much more will visible things be understood by means of invisible by those who advance in spiritual contemplation. Indeed, the symbolic contemplation of intelligible things by means of visible realities is spiritual knowledge and understanding of visible things through the visible. For it is necessary that things which manifest each other bear a mutual reflection in an altogether true and clear manner and keep their relationship intact.

Chapter Eight
Of what the first entrance of the holy synaxis and
the ceremonies which follow it are symbols.

After the concise exposition of the views expressed by the blessed old man concerning holy Church, our discourse can proceed by making an even briefer interpretation, as we can, of

Here again we see the importance of the concept of the image (symbol, type, figure) for Maximus. The levels of being are held together through the relationship of image to archetype. So also, Maximus implies, is the "big" chasm with which he begins his treatise — the separation between God and creation — overcome. Again, Maximus uses language developed at the Council of Chalcedon. As the divine and human natures are held together in the one Christ in an unconfused but also undivided way, so too are the diverse parts of the one world.

3. See Ezekiel 1:15-21.

Maximus again uses the symbolism of the church building. The nave is earth and the enclosed area around the altar table, heaven. The bishop's throne was at the top of a set of stone steps in the apse behind the altar table. Notice the importance of the procession and the interpretation of the action by the Gospel story.

the holy synaxis. According to his teaching, then, the first entrance of the bishop into the holy Church for the sacred synaxis is a figure and image of the first appearance in the flesh of Jesus Christ, the son of God and our Savior in this world. By it he freed human nature, which had been enslaved by corruption, betrayed through its own fault to death because of sin, tyrannically dominated by the devil. He redeemed all its debt as if he were liable even though he was not liable but sinless, and brought us back again to the original grace of his kingdom by giving himself as a ransom for us. And in exchange for our destructive passions he gives us his life-giving Passion as a salutary cure which saves the whole world. After this appearance, his **ascension** into heaven and return to the heavenly throne are symbolically figured in the bishop's entrance into the sanctuary and ascent to the priestly throne.

Chapter Nine
What is the meaning of the entrance of the people into the holy church of God.

Unlike other liturgical traditions in which the people waited inside the church for the clergy, in the Byzantine tradition people entered the church with the clergy.

The venerable old man used to say that the entrance of the people into the church with the bishop represents the conversion of the unfaithful from faithlessness to faith and from sin and error to the recognition of God as well as the passage of the faithful from vice and ignorance to virtue and knowledge. For entrance into the church signifies not only the conversion of infidels to the true and only God but also the amendment of each one of us who believe but who yet violate the Lord's commandments under the influence of a loose and indecent life. Indeed, when any person is a murderer, or adulterer, robber, haughty, boastful, insolent, ambitious, greedy, slanderous, resentful, inclined to outbursts and anger, a drunkard, and in a word — lest I weary my discourse by enumerating all kinds of vice — when someone is entangled in any kind of vice but should cease voluntarily to be held by its attention and deliberately to act according to it and changes his life for the better by preferring virtue to vice, such a person can be properly and truly considered and spoken of as entering with Christ our God and High Priest into virtue, which is the church understood figuratively.

Chapter Ten
What is symbolized by the divine readings.

Maximus goes through the order of worship several times, each time pointing to a different level of meaning. Here he focuses on the meaning for individual believers. The liturgy, especially through the Bible readings and their exposition in the sermon, provides instruction for Christian living.

The master used to say that the divine readings from the sacred books reveal the divine and blessed desires and intentions of God most holy. Through them each one of us receives in proportion to the capacity which is in him the counsels by which he should act, and we learn the laws of the divine and blessed struggles in which by consistent fighting we will be judged worthy of the victorious crowns of Christ's kingdom.[4]

4. See 1 Corinthians 9:24-25; 2 Timothy 4:7-9; James 1:12.

Chapter Eleven
What the divine chants symbolize.

He used to say that the spiritual enjoyment of the divine hymns signified the vivid delights of the divine blessings by moving souls toward the clear and blessed love of God and by arousing them further to the hatred of sin.

The hymns were the psalms and refrains sung before each reading.

Chapter Twelve
What the salutations of peace signify.

The wise man declared that by the salutations of peace which are issued from within the sanctuary on the signal of the bishop at each reading are indicated the divine favors imparted by the holy angels. By them God determines the combats of those who fight bravely for the truth against opposing forces by breaking off the invisible struggles and by giving peace in the destruction of the body and by giving to the saints the grace of detachment in return for their labors for virtue. And once delivered from this warfare, they turn the forces of the soul to spiritual cultivation, that is, to the accomplishment of the virtues. Through these forces they disperse the armies of evil spirits under the command of God the Word, who scatters the sharp and wily machinations of the devil.

The salutations were blessings given by the bishop at each Scripture reading in the first part of the service. The gesture of blessing was probably like Christ's in the icon on p. 34.

Chapter Thirteen
Of what specifically are the reading of the holy Gospel and the mysteries that follow it a symbol.

Immediately after these things the sacred order of the holy Church prescribes that there should take place the reading of the divine Gospel which specifically proposes to those who are zealous some suffering on behalf of the Word. Then the word of **gnostic** contemplation comes to them from heaven as High Priest to constrict their fleshly understanding as a sort of sensible world by restraining the reasoning still inclining to earth, and in driving them away from there it leads them, by the closing of the doors and the entrance into the **holy mysteries**, to the vision of spiritual principles and realities. And after having shut their senses and having become outside of the flesh and the world, he teaches them unspeakable things as they are reconciled first with each other and with him through the kiss of peace and offer him in return for his numerous benefits toward them the grateful confession for their salvation which is intimated by the creed of faith. Next, having set them in the number of the angels through the **Trisagion**[5] and having bestowed on them the same understanding of sanctifying theology as theirs, he leads them to God the Father, having become adopted in the Spirit

The "word" coming from heaven was symbolized by the Gospel reading and also by the bishop as he descended from his throne to dismiss the catechumens and begin the Liturgy of the Faithful (see pp. 86-92). By "gnostic contemplation," Maximus means contemplation of "the things of the Spirit" (see Romans 8:15).

Maximus highlights the desired effect of the sermon: to wean the worshipers from attachment to this world for adhesion to the heavenly, demonstrated by unity in faith manifested in worship through the kiss of peace and the recitation of the Creed.

5. See Isaiah 6:3; the "Trisagion" ("Thrice Holy") is the "Holy, Holy, Holy" sung during the Eucharistic prayer and based on the song of the seraphim.

The problem posed in the introduction — that God is unknowable and unapproachable by nature — is overcome as Christ leads the faithful "beyond knowledge to the unknowable" God, whom they know intimately through personal relationship. Commenting on "One Is Holy," Maximus chooses *Monad* from Greek philosophy, meaning "Oneness" or "Unity," as a term for God.

Maximus shifts his interpretation from its connection to specific worshipers to general reference to the story of the church and its fulfillment in the end times.

After the dismissal of the unbaptized, only the baptized are present for the latter part of the service. With the bishop's descent, he is on the same level with the congregation as together they enter through the Lord's Supper into "the nuptial chamber," i.e., heavenly intimacy with God in Christ.

through the prayer whereby they were rendered worthy to call God Father. And again after that, as having through knowledge passed all the principles in beings, he leads them beyond knowledge to the unknowable **Monad** by the hymn "One Is Holy," and so forth; now divinized by love and made like him by participation in an indivisible identity to the extent that this is possible.

Chapter Fourteen
Of what the divine reading of the holy Gospel is a symbol in its general meaning. What is generally intimated about the end of this world.

After the divine reading of the holy Gospel the bishop descends from his throne and there takes place the dismissal and sending away of the catechumens and of others unworthy of the divine vision of the mysteries to be displayed. It signifies and figures by itself the truth, of which it is an image and figure, as if proclaiming thereby that after having preached, as is written, "the Gospel of the kingdom in the whole world as a witness to all the Gentiles" [Matt. 24:14], the end will then appear in the second coming of our great God and Savior Jesus Christ from the heavens in glory. "For the Lord himself . . . will come down from heaven at the archangel's voice and the Lord's trumpet," says the divine Apostle [1 Thess. 4:16]. And he will wreak vengeance on his enemies and through the holy angels will separate the faithful from the unfaithful, the just from the unjust, the saints from the accursed, and, in short, those who have walked uprightly in the Spirit of God from those who follow after the flesh,[6] and for infinite and endless ages, as the truth of God's declarations affirms, he will render to each one the just reward of the life he has led.[7]

Chapter Fifteen
Of what the closing of the doors of the holy church after the reading of the holy Gospel is a symbol.

The closing of the doors which takes place after the sacred reading of the holy Gospel and the dismissal of the catechumens signifies the passing from material things which will come about after that terrible separation and even more terrible judgment and the entrance of those who are worthy into the spiritual world, that is, into the nuptial chamber of Christ, as well as the complete extinction in our senses of deceptive activity.

6. See Matthew 24:31; Matthew 13:49; Romans 8:4-8.
7. See Romans 2:6.

Chapter Sixteen
What is signified by the entrance into the holy mysteries.

The entrance into the holy and august mysteries, as that great old man used to say, is the beginning and prelude of the new teaching which will take place in the heavens concerning the plan of God for us and the revelation of the mystery of our salvation,[8] which is in the most secret recesses of the divine.

For as the Word of God says to his disciples, "I shall not drink of the fruit of the vine until that day when I drink it anew with you in the kingdom of my Father" [Matt. 26:29].

Chapter Seventeen
What is symbolized by the divine kiss.

The spiritual kiss which is extended to all prefigures and portrays the concord, unanimity, and identity of views which we shall all have among ourselves in faith and love at the time of the revelation of the ineffable blessings to come. In this situation those who are worthy will receive intimate familiarity with the Word of God. For the mouth is a symbol of the Word, precisely through whom all those who share in reason as reasonable beings are united to the first and unique Word, who is the cause of every word and meaning.

Chapter Eighteen
What is symbolized by the divine symbol of faith.

The profession by all of the divine symbol of faith signifies the mystical thanksgiving to perdure through all eternity for the marvelous principles and modes by which we were saved by God's all-wise Providence on our behalf. Through it those who are worthy are confirmed as grateful for the divine favors, for otherwise they would have no other way of returning anything at all for the numberless divine blessings toward them.

Chapter Nineteen
What is symbolized by the doxology of the Trisagion.

The triple exclamation of holiness which all the faithful people proclaim in the divine hymn represents the union and the equality of honor to be manifested in the future with the incorporeal and intelligent powers. In this state human nature, in harmony with the powers on high through the identity of an inflexible, eternal movement around God, will be taught to sing and to proclaim holy with a triple holiness the single Godhead in three Persons.

8. See Ephesians 1:8-10; Colossians 1:26, 2:2-3.

The **"holy mysteries"** refers first of all to the bread and wine of the Eucharist, and then more generally to the Liturgy of the Faithful. The phrase "entrance into the holy mysteries" may also be translated "entrance **of** the holy mysteries," in which case it refers more specifically to the procession with the bread and wine.

According to Basil the Great (4th century), recounting the Trinity's wonders could be a way of glorifying God (*On the Holy Spirit*, 54). Thus, reciting the Creed was thanksgiving. Although it may seem that the Eucharistic prayer, which also recounts salvation history (see pp. 94-95 and p. 101), should have this role, this prayer began to be recited silently in the sixth century (see p. 134), leaving the people with only the Creed for their thanksgiving.

The "Holy, Holy, Holy" is the only part of the Eucharistic prayer that Maximus comments on. This is probably because this hymn was one of the few parts accessible to laypeople like himself.

Chapter Twenty

Of what the holy prayer "Our Father" is a symbol.

The most holy and venerable invocation of our great and blessed God the Father is a symbol of the personal and real adoption to be bestowed through the gift and grace of the Holy Spirit.[9] In accordance with it, once every human particularity is overcome and disclosed by the coming of grace, all the saints will be and be called sons of God to the extent that from that moment they will have radiantly and gloriously brightened themselves through the virtues with the divine beauty of goodness.

Chapter Twenty-One

What is signified by the conclusion of the mystical service when the hymns are sung, that is, "One Is Holy," and so forth.

In these chapters we see the importance of theology for the Byzantine understanding of salvation. Just as there is unity in diversity in the Trinity (Chapter 19), saved people will experience unity in diversity as children of God by grace (Chapter 20). As in the Incarnation the whole of divine nature fills the whole of human nature in the one person of Christ (Chapter 2), a similar thing happens in the relationship of humans with God (Chapter 21), though this is a relationship not of natures but of persons. The human person is not lost or absorbed but, as Maximus says in Chapter 23, "transformed unchangeably."

The profession "One Is Holy" and what follows, which is voiced by all the people at the end of the mystical service, represents the gathering and union beyond reason and understanding which will take place between those who have been mystically and wisely initiated by God and the mysterious oneness of the divine simplicity in the incorruptible age of the spiritual world. There they behold the light of the invisible and ineffable glory and become themselves, together with the angels on high, open to the blessed purity. After this, as the climax of everything, comes the distribution of the sacrament, which transforms into itself and renders similar to the causal good by grace and participation those who worthily share in it. To them is there lacking nothing of this good that is possible and attainable for men,[10] so that they also can be and be called gods by adoption through grace because all of God entirely fills them and leaves no part of them empty of his presence.

Chapter Twenty-Four

What mysteries the enduring grace of the Holy Spirit effects and brings to completion through the rites accomplished in the holy synaxis in the faithful and those gathered in the church out of faith.

This, indeed, is why the blessed old man believed that every Christian should be exhorted — and he never failed to do this — to frequent God's holy Church and never to abandon the holy synaxis accomplished therein because of the holy angels who remain there and who take note each time people enter and present themselves to God, and they make supplications for them; likewise because of the grace of the Holy Spirit, which is always invisibly present, but in

---

9. See Galatians 4:4-7.
10. Here and elsewhere in this text the Greek term translated "man" or "men" is better translated "human being(s)." There is no intentional reference to a particular sex.

a special way at the time of the holy synaxis. This grace transforms and changes each person who is found there and in fact remolds him in proportion to what is more divine in him and leads him to what is revealed through the mysteries which are celebrated, even if he does not himself feel this because he is still among those who are children in Christ, unable to see either into the depths of the reality or the grace operating in it, which is revealed through each of the divine symbols of salvation being accomplished, and which proceeds according to the order and progression from preliminaries to the end of everything.

Thus we see effected in the first entrance the rejection of unbelief, the increase of faith, the lessening of vice, the bestowal of virtue, the disappearance of ignorance, and the development of knowledge. By the hearing of the divine words there is effected the firm and unchangeable habits and dispositions of the realities just mentioned, that is, of faith, virtue, and knowledge. Through the divine chants which follow there is effected the deliberate consent of the soul to virtue as well as the spiritual delight and enjoyment that these arouse in it. By the sacred reading of the holy Gospel there is brought about the end of earthly thinking, as of the world of sense. Then by the closing of doors which follows there is effected the passage and transfer of the soul in its disposition from this corruptible world to the intelligible world, whereby having closed its senses like doors it renders them cleansed of the idols of sin. By the entrance into the holy mysteries we see the more perfect and mystical and new teaching and knowledge of God's dispensation toward us. By the divine kiss there is seen the identity of concord and oneness and love of all with everyone and of each one with himself first and then with God. By the profession of the symbol of faith there is seen the fitting thanks for the marvelous ways of our salvation. By the Trisagion there comes about the union with the holy angels and elevation to the same honor, as well as the ceaseless and harmonious persistency in the sanctifying glorification of God. By the prayer through which we are made worthy to call God our Father, we receive the truest adoption in the grace of the Holy Spirit. By the "One Is Holy" and what follows, we have the grace and familiarity which unites us to God himself. By holy communion of the spotless and life-giving mysteries, we are given fellowship and identity with him by participation in likeness, by which man is deemed worthy from man to become God. For we believe that in this present life we already have a share in these gifts of the Holy Spirit through the love that is in faith, and in the future age, after we have kept the commandments to the best of our ability, we believe that we shall have a share in them in very truth in their concrete reality according to the steadfast hope of our faith and the solid and unchangeable promise to which God has committed himself. Then we shall pass from the grace which is in faith to the grace of vision, when our God and Savior Jesus Christ will indeed transform us into himself by taking away from us the marks of corruption and will bestow on us the original mysteries which have been represented for us through sensible symbols here below. To make it easier to remember, if you wish let us recapitulate thus the meaning of what has been said by running over it briefly.

In this succinct summary we can clearly see the Order of Worship for the communion service as it existed in Maximus's time (items in parentheses are implied):

- Entrance into Church
- Readings
- Psalm Chants
- Gospel
- (Catechumens Dismissed)
- Closing of Doors
- Procession with Gifts
- Kiss of Peace
- Creed
- (Eucharistic Prayer)
- "Holy, Holy, Holy"
- Lord's Prayer
- (Call to Communion)
- "One Is Holy"
- Communion

Again we are reminded how valuable this treatise is for the history of worship.

Maximus's interpretation of worship allows any one aspect to have multiple points of reference. Here he summarizes by repeating each meaning he has discovered in each part of worship. Maximus distinguishes between general meanings, which indicate the church as a whole, and particular meanings, which concern individual Christians. He also finds different meanings for people at different stages of spiritual development, for the "active" and for "those who have knowledge," i.e., contemplatives. For some writers, active and contemplative define different approaches to life. For Maximus, however, they must exist together in the same person. By practicing virtue, people come to know the truth of God.

Thus the holy Church, as we said, is the figure and image of God inasmuch as through it he effects in his infinite power and wisdom an unconfused unity from the various essences of beings, attaching them to himself as a creator at their highest point, and this operates according to the grace of faith for the faithful, joining them all to each other in one form according to a single grace and calling of faith, the active and virtuous ones in a single identity of will, the contemplative and gnostic ones in an unbroken and undivided concord as well. It is a figure of both the spiritual and the sensible world, with the sanctuary as symbol of the intelligible world and the nave as symbol of the world of sense.

It is as well an image of man inasmuch as it represents the soul by the sanctuary and suggests the body by the nave. Also, it is a figure and image of the soul considered in itself because by the sanctuary it bears the glory of the contemplative element and by the nave the ornament of the active part. The first entrance of the holy synaxis which is celebrated in the church signifies in general the first appearance of Christ our God, and in particular the conversion of those who are being led by him and with him from unbelief to faith and from vice to virtue and also from ignorance to knowledge. The readings which take place after it signify in general the divine wishes and intentions in accordance with which everyone should conform and conduct himself, and in particular the teaching and progress in the faith of those who are believers, and the firm disposition of virtue of those who are active in accordance with which, by submitting themselves to the divine law of the commandments, they set themselves bravely and unshakenly against the devil's wiles and escape his adversary works; finally, it signifies the contemplative habits of those who have knowledge, in accordance with which, by bringing together as much as possible the spiritual principles of sensible realities and of Providence in what concerns them, they are borne without error to the truth.

The divine melodies of the chants indicate the divine delight and enjoyment which comes about in the souls of all. By it they are mystically strengthened in forgetting their past labors for virtue and are renewed in the vigorous desire of the divine and wholesome benefits still to be attained.

The holy Gospel is in general a symbol of the fulfillment of this world; in particular, it indicates the complete disappearance of the ancient error in those who have believed; in the active, the mortification and the end of the law and thinking according to the flesh; and in those who have knowledge, the gathering and ascent from the numerous and various principles toward the most comprehensive principle, once the most detailed and varied natural contemplation has been reached and crossed.

The descent of the bishop from the throne and the dismissal of the catechumens signifies in general the second coming from heaven of our great God and Savior Jesus Christ and the separation of sinners from the saints and the just retribution rendered to each. In particular it means the perfect assurance of believers in faith which is produced by the Word of God become invisibly present to them, whereby every thought which still limps in some way regarding faith is dismissed from them, as are the catechumens. Thus for the active ones there results perfect detachment by which every passionate and unenlightened thought departs from the soul, and for those with knowledge the comprehensive science of whatever is known by which all images of material things are chased away from the soul.

The closing of the doors and the entrance into the holy mysteries and the divine kiss and the recitation of the symbol of faith mean in general the passing away of sensible things and the appearance of spiritual realities and the new teaching of the divine mystery involving us and the future concord, unanimity, love, and identity of everyone with each other and with God, as well as the thanksgiving for the manner of our salvation. In a particular way it means the progress of the faithful from simple faith to learning in dogmas, initiation, accord, and piety. The closing of the doors indicates the first thing, the entrance into the holy actions the second, the kiss the third, the recitation of the creed the fourth. For those at the active stage, it means the transfer from activity to contemplation of those who have closed their senses and who have become outside the flesh and the world by the rejection of activities for their own sake, and the ascent from the mode of the commandments to their principle, and the connatural kinship and union of these commandments in their proper principles with the powers of the soul and the habit which is adapted to theological thanksgiving. For those who have knowledge, it involves the passing of natural contemplation to the simple understanding according to which they no longer pursue the divine and ineffable Word by sensation or anything that appears and the union with the soul of its powers and the simplicity which takes in under one form by the intellect the principle of Providence.

The unceasing and sanctifying doxology by the holy angels in the Trisagion signifies, in general, the equality in the way of life and conduct and the harmony in the divine praising which will take place in the age to come by both heavenly and earthly powers, when the human body now rendered immortal by the resurrection will no longer weigh down the soul by corruption and will not itself be weighed down but will take on, by the change into incorruption, potency and aptitude to receive God's coming. In particular it signifies, for the faithful, the theological rivalry with the angels in faith; for the active ones, it symbolizes the splendor of life equal to [that of] the angels, so far as this is possible for men, and the persistence in the theological hymnology; for those who have knowledge, endless thoughts, hymns, and movements concerning the Godhead which are equal to [those of] the angels, so far as humanly possible.

The blessed invocation of the great God and Father and the acclamation of the "One Is Holy" and what follows and the partaking of the holy and life-giving mysteries signify the adoption and union, as well as the familiarity and divine likeness and deification, which will come about through the goodness of our God in every way on all the worthy, whereby God himself will be "all in all" alike to those who are saved as a pattern of beauty resplendent as a cause in those who are resplendent along with him in grace by virtue and knowledge.

Like other patristic writers, Maximus distinguishes levels of spiritual growth on the basis of motive, whether Christians obey out of fear of punishment, desire for spiritual rewards, or love of God.

He used to call faithful, virtuous, and knowing the beginners, the proficient, and the perfect, that is, slaves, mercenaries, and sons, the three classes of the saved. The slaves are the faithful who execute the Lord's commandments out of fear of threats and who willingly work for those who are obeyed. Mercenaries are those who out of a desire for promised benefits bear with patience "the burden and heat of the day," that is, the affliction innate in and yoked to the present life from the condemnation of our first parents, and the temptations from it on behalf of virtue, and who by free choice of will wisely exchange life for life, the present one for the future. Finally, sons are the ones who out of neither fear of threats nor desire of promised things but rather out of character and habit of the voluntary inclination and disposition of the soul toward the good never become separated from God, as that son to whom it was said, "Son, you are always with me, and everything I have is yours" [Luke 15:31]. They have become as much as possible by deification in grace what God is and is believed by nature and by cause.

Having summarized the symbolic significance of the liturgy, Maximus concludes with the consequences for living. The liturgy manifests a relationship with God that must be lived out.

Let us, then, not stray from the holy Church of God which comprehends, in the sacred order of the divine symbols which are celebrated, such great mysteries of our salvation. Through them, in making each of us who conducts himself worthily as best he can in Christ, it brings to light the grace of adoption, which was given through holy baptism in the Holy Spirit and which makes us perfect in Christ. Instead, let us with all our strength and zeal render ourselves worthy of the divine gifts in pleasing God by good works, not being occupied as are "the pagans who know not God," with "the passion of concupiscence," but as the holy Apostle says, "putting to death our members which are rooted in earth: fornication, impurity, passion, evil desire and covetousness which is idolatry, from which comes God's wrath on the sons of disobedience, and all wrath, animosity, foul language, and lying, and to sum up, putting aside the old man which is corrupted by the lusts of illusion with his past deeds and lusts, let us walk in a manner worthy of God who has called us to his kingdom and his glory, having clothed ourselves with heartfelt compassion, with kindness, humility, meekness, and patience, bearing with one another in love and forgiving one another if one has a complaint against the other, just as Christ has forgiven us, and over all these let us clothe ourselves with love and peace, the bond of perfection, to which we have been called in one body, in short, the new man who is constantly renewed in full knowledge according to the image of the one who created him."[11] For if we lived in this way, we would be able to arrive at the goal of the divine promises with a good hope and to be filled "with the knowledge of his will in all wisdom and spiritual understanding, . . . being fruitful and increasing in the knowledge of the Lord, strengthened with all power according to the might of his glory for edification and long-suffering with joy, giving thanks to the Father for having made us worthy to share the inheritance of the saints in the light" [Col. 1:9-12].

11. Maximus combines several of Paul's exhortations: 1 Thessalonians 4:5; Colossians 3:5-6, 8-9; Ephesians 4:22; 1 Thessalonians 2:12; and Colossians 3:12-14, 10.

The clear proof of this grace is the voluntary disposition of good will toward those akin to us whereby the man who needs our help in any way becomes as much as possible our friend as God is, and we do not leave him abandoned and forsaken but rather with fitting zeal we show him in action the disposition which is alive in us with respect to God and our neighbor. For a work is proof of a disposition. Now nothing is either so fitting for justification or so apt for divinization, if I can speak thus, and nearness to God as mercy offered with pleasure and joy from the soul to those who stand in need. For if the Word has shown that the one who is in need of having good done to him is God — for as long, he tells us, as you did it for one of these least ones, you did it for me[12] — on God's very word, then, he will much more show that the one who can do good and who does it is truly God by grace and participation because he has taken on in happy imitation the energy and characteristic of his own doing good. And if the poor man is God, it is because of God's condescension in becoming poor for us and in taking upon himself by his own suffering the sufferings of each one and "until the end of time," always suffering mystically out of goodness in proportion to each one's suffering. All the more reason, then, will that one be God who by loving men in imitation of God heals by himself in divine fashion the hurts of those who suffer and who shows that he has in his disposition, safeguarding all proportion, the same power of saving Providence that God has.

Who, then, is so slow and lazy with regard to virtue as not to desire divinity when one can acquire it at such small cost and so readily and easily? For a firm and secure protection of these things and an easy way to salvation, outside of which none of these benefits will be kept truly without harm by the one who has them, is the personal attention to our actions whereby in learning to regard and consider what concerns us alone we free ourselves from the hollow hurt caused by others. For if we learn to see and examine ourselves alone, we will never interfere in another's concerns, whatever they might be, because we acknowledge God as the only wise and just judge who judges wisely and justly all things that exist according to the principle of their being, not according to the manner of their appearance. Men might also make a judgment by looking vaguely at appearances, but the truth and meaning of existing things are not at all to be found there. God, on the other hand, who looks at the soul's hidden motivation and its unseen desire and the principle of these by which the soul is drawn, and its goal, that is, the foreseen end of every action, judges rightly, as was said, all the actions of men. And if we are zealous in succeeding in this and stay within our limited compass without becoming involved in external things, we shall not permit the eye, ear, or tongue either to see, hear, or speak at all, if possible, what is the business of others, or at least in getting involved with compassion rather than with passion, we allow ourselves to see, hear, and speak them for our profit and only insofar as it seems good to the divine word who controls them. For nothing slips more easily toward sin than these organs when they are not disciplined by

The "disposition with respect to God and our neighbor" is love (see Matt. 22:34-40), which for Maximus must be manifested in action.

Maximus presents the full significance for life of the "Incarnational principle." The human sufferer is God because God identifies with the sufferer by "condescending" in the Incarnation to participate fully in human life. The human person who works to alleviate suffering takes part in God's healing activity by imitation and thus will enjoy divine life "by grace and participation."

The correlative of "Love thy neighbor" is "Judge not."

12. See Matthew 25:45.

reason, and on the other hand, nothing is more apt to salvation when it commands, controls, and leads them toward where it ought and chooses to go.

Therefore, let us to the best of our ability not be careless in obeying God, who calls us to eternal life and to a blessed end through the observance of his divine and saving commandments "to receive mercy and find grace as an aid in time of need" [Heb. 4:16]. "For grace," says the divine Apostle, "is with all who love our Lord Jesus Christ in incorruptibility" [Eph. 6:24], that is, those who love our Lord with the incorruptibility of virtue and the pure and sincere dignity of life, or, to speak more clearly, those who love the Lord by doing his will and by not transgressing any of his commands.[13]

13. See John 15:10.

Source: The *Mystagogy* of Maximus the Confessor is found in a recent English translation by George Berthold: *Maximus Confessor: Selected Writings,* Classics of Western Spirituality (Mahwah, N.J.: Paulist Press, 1985). Berthold based his English translation on the original Greek found in this edition: C. Soteropoulos, *Mystagogy* (Athens, 1978). Text copyright 1985 by George Berthold. Paulist Press, Inc., New York/Mahwah, N.J. The excerpts that appear here are reprinted by permission of Paulist Press, Inc. www.paulistpress.com.

Eutychius's Comments on Sixth-Century Byzantine Worship

In the following excerpt from an Easter-time sermon, Eutychius, Constantinople's bishop from 552-65 and 577-82, complains about the popular reverence shown to the bread and wine as they are brought forward for consecration in communion. His complaint is that the people have begun their worship of Christ too early, since the food is still plain food before the Eucharistic prayer. Eutychius's complaint shows his understanding of the importance of the Great Prayer of Thanks-giving said to consecrate the Eucharist. In general, however, Byzantine piety and worship resist the kind of precision that Eutychius wants to bring to them. It is also interesting that the bishop is at odds with his people about what constitutes appropriate worship. In particular, Eutychius complains about the Cherubic Hymn, which had been introduced by a rival a few years before his second tenure as Patriarch.[1] Yet he does not change or eliminate the hymn. Perhaps, at times, we overestimate the bishop's power and underestimate popular initiatives in ancient worship.

They act stupidly, who have taught the people to sing a certain psalmic chant when the ministers are about to bring up to the altar the bread of oblation and the recently mixed chalice. In this hymn, which they consider suitable to the action being performed, the people say that they bear in the king of glory and refer in this way to the things being brought up, even though they have not yet been consecrated by the high-priestly invocation — unless perhaps what is sung means something else to them. For as Athanasius the Great says in his sermon to the baptized: "You will see the Levites [i.e., deacons] bearing in breads and a chalice of wine and putting them on the table. And as long as the supplications and prayers have not been completed, it is nothing but plain bread."

This procession with the elements for communion was (and remains) one of the key movements in the worship space. All the food which would have been brought for communion would have first been gathered in a separate building called a **skeuophylakion**. From there it was brought to the altar during the Liturgy of the Faithful. This sermon gives us a sense of the importance that this procession had already attained by the sixth century.

1. Robert Taft is probably right that the phrase "King of glory" comes from Psalm 24, which was chanted with the Cherubic Hymn (*The Great Entrance* [Rome: Pontifical Oriental Institute, 1978], p. 85). But it is more likely that Eutychius would complain about the new practice of singing the hymn rather than the more ancient practice of chanting the psalm. It is through the hymn that the people, who "represent the cherubim," can be seen to play a role in bringing the King, "escorted by the angelic hosts," to the altar table. For the text of this hymn and the way it was likely used in the sixth century, see "A Reconstruction of the Order of a Divine Liturgy of Saint Basil," on p. 83.

Source: The sermon excerpt from Patriarch Eutychius of Constantinople, from his sermon entitled *Sermo de paschate et de ss. eucharistia,* is from Robert F. Taft, *The Great Entrance* (Rome: Pontifical Oriental Institute, 1978), pp. 84-85 (excerpt used by permission). Taft translates the sermon as found in *Patrologia graeca* 86 (2), 2400-2401.

Procopius's Description of the Splendor of Hagia Sophia

In a work that sought to magnify the work of the emperor Justinian, the sixth-century Byzantine historian Procopius speaks of the grandeur of the newly built Hagia Sophia. His account is significant because it is the only one extant that describes the church before the collapse of the original dome in 558. Works like this one and the one that follows by Paul the Silentiary help us understand how people of the time experienced the church. We must also remember, however, that this is an idealized portrayal of the building.

So the church has become a spectacle of marvelous beauty, overwhelming to those who see it, but to those who know it by hearsay altogether incredible. For it soars to a height to match the sky, and as if surging up from amongst the other buildings it stands on high and looks down upon the remainder of the city, adorning it, because it is a part of it, but glorying in its own beauty, because, though a part of the city and dominating it, it at the same time towers above it to such a height that the whole city is viewed from there as from a watchtower. Both its breadth and its length have been so carefully proportioned that it may not improperly be said to be exceedingly long and at the same time unusually broad. And it exults in an indescribable beauty.

For it proudly reveals its mass and the harmony of its proportions, having neither any excess nor deficiency, since it is both more pretentious than the buildings to which we are accustomed, and considerably more noble than those which are merely huge, and it abounds exceedingly in sunlight and in the reflection of the sun's rays from the marble. Indeed, one might say that its interior is not illuminated from without by the sun, but that the radiance comes into being within it, such an abundance of light bathes this shrine. And the face itself of the church (which would be the part which faces the rising sun, that portion of the building in which they perform the mysteries in worship of God) was constructed in the following manner. A structure of masonry is built up from the ground, not made in a straight line, but gradually curving inward on its flanks and receding at the middle, so that it forms the shape of half a circle, which those who are skilled in such matters call a half-cylinder; and so it rises precipitously to a height. The upper part of this structure ends in the fourth part of a sphere, and above it another crescent-shaped structure rises, fitted to the adjoining parts of the building, marvelous in its grace, but by reason of the seeming insecurity of its composition altogether terrifying. For it seems somehow to float in the air on no firm basis, but to be poised aloft to the peril of those inside it. Yet actually it is braced with exceptional firmness and security. On either side of this are columns arranged on the pavement; these likewise do not stand in a straight line, but they retreat inward in the pattern of the semicircle as if they were yielding to one another in a choral dance, and above them hangs a structure of crescent shape. And on the side opposite the east is reared a wall

Hagia Sophia is lit by sunlight. The effect, however, suggests something different, a manifesting of the light of God's glory from within. At the beginning of the service, the worshiper feels that she or he is proceeding with all the faithful into the heavenly realm bathed with God's light. The reader should hear allusions to biblical stories of glory-endued enlightenment or transfiguration. Behind Procopius's astonishment, too, is an ancient Christian sensibility that a goal in worship is to be able to see truly or rightly.

containing the entrances, and on either side of this there stand in a semicircle not only the columns themselves but also the structure above them, all this being very similar to the columns and structure I have just described. And in the center of the church stand four man-made eminences, which they call piers, two on the north side and two on the south, opposite and equal to each other, each pair having between them just four columns. The piers are composed of huge stones joined together, carefully selected and skillfully fitted to one another by the masons, and rising to a great height. One might suppose that they were sheer mountain-peaks. From these spring four arches which rise over the four sides of a square, and their ends come together in pairs and are made fast to each other on top of these piers, while the other portions rise and soar to an infinite height. And while two of the arches rise over empty air, those namely on the east and the west sides, the other two have under them certain structural elements, including a number of rather small columns. Upon the crowns of the arches rests a circular structure, cylindrical in shape; it is through this that the light of day always first smiles. For it towers above the whole earth, as I believe, and the structure is interrupted at short intervals, openings having been left intentionally, in the spaces where the perforation of the stone-work takes place, to be channels for the admission of light in sufficient measure. And since the arches where they are joined together are so constructed as to form a four-cornered plan, the stonework between the arches produces four triangles. And while each supporting end of a triangle, having been contracted to a point by the coming together of each pair of arches, makes the lower point an acute angle, yet as the triangle rises and its width is extended by the intermediate surface, it ends in the segment of a circle which it supports, and forms the remaining angles at that level. And upon this circle rests the huge spherical dome which makes the structure exceptionally beautiful. Yet it seems not to rest upon solid masonry, but to cover the space with its golden dome suspended from Heaven. All these details, fitted together with incredible skill in mid-air and floating off from each other and resting only on the parts next to them, produce a single and most extraordinary harmony in the work, and yet do not permit the spectator to linger much over the study of any one of them, but each detail attracts the eye and draws it on irresistibly to itself. So the vision constantly shifts suddenly, for the beholder is utterly unable to select which particular detail he should admire more than all the others. But even so, though they turn their attention to every side and look with contracted brows upon every detail, observers are still unable to understand the skillful craftsmanship, but they always depart from there overwhelmed by the bewildering sight. So much, then, for this.

It was by many skillful devices that the emperor Justinian and the master-builders Anthemius and Isidorus secured the stability of the church, hanging, as it does, in mid-air. Some of these it is both hopeless for me to understand in their entirety, and impossible to explain in words; I shall record only one of them for the present, from which it should be possible to

The construction of magnificent buildings which awe and show the beauty of God's holiness has been a recurring event in Christian worship history. This tendency contrasts with the earlier, more humble domestic setting for worship as well as with some later Christian traditions which have intentionally built simple spaces to emphasize the people.

Just as with the light, which appears unearthly, the height, size, and seemingly heaven-like suspension of the main dome create a sense of being in heaven.

Procopius pauses to admire the human ingenuity which produced such an engineering marvel. Indeed, Justinian's church was in many respects an architectural breakthrough that remains without parallel.

gain an impression of the strength of the whole work. It is as follows: The piers which I have just mentioned are not constructed in the same way as other structures, but in the following manner. The courses of stone were laid down so as to form a four-cornered shape, the stones being rough by nature but worked smooth; and they were cut to the angles when they were destined to form the projecting corners of the sides of the pier, but when they chanced to be assigned to a position between the angles, they were cut in rectangles. These were held together neither by lime, which they call "asbestus," nor by asphalt, the material which was the pride of Semiramis in Babylon, nor by any other such thing, but by lead poured into the interstices, which flowed about everywhere in the spaces between the stones and hardened in the joints, binding them to each other. Thus were these parts constructed; but let us proceed to the remaining portions of the church.

The whole ceiling is overlaid with pure gold, which adds glory to the beauty, yet the light reflected from the stones prevails, shining out in rivalry with the gold. And there are two stoa-like colonnades [i.e., like covered walkways or porticos], one on each side, not separated in any way from the structure of the church itself, but actually making the effect of its width greater, and reaching along its whole length, to the very end, while in height they are less than the interior of the building. And they too have vaulted ceilings and decorations of gold. One of these two colonnaded stoas [porticos] has been assigned to men worshipers, while the other is reserved for women engaged in the same exercise. But they have nothing to distinguish them, nor do they differ from one another in any way, but their very equality serves to beautify the church, and their similarity to adorn it. But who could fittingly describe the galleries of the women's side, or enumerate the many colonnades and the colonnaded aisles by means of which the church is surrounded? Or who could recount the beauty of the columns and the stones with which the church is adorned? One might imagine that he had come upon a meadow with its flowers in full bloom. For he would surely marvel at the purple of some, the green tint of others, and at those on which the crimson glows and those from which the white flashes, and again at those which Nature, like some painter, varies with the most contrasting colors. And whenever anyone enters this church to pray, he understands at once that it is not by any human power or skill, but by the influence of God, that this work has been so finely turned. And so his mind is lifted up toward God and exalted, feeling that He cannot be far away, but must especially love to dwell in this place which He has chosen. And this does not happen only to one who sees the church for the first time, but the same experience comes to him on each successive occasion, as though the sight were new each time. Of this spectacle no one has ever had a surfeit, but when present in the church, men rejoice in what they see, and when they leave it, they take proud delight in conversing about it. Furthermore, concerning the treasures of this church — the vessels of gold and silver and the works in precious stones, which the emperor Justinian has dedicated here — it is impossible to give a precise account of them

The aisles under the galleries or balconies, separated from the main nave of the church by columns, remind Procopius of porticos, the covered sidewalks that lined Constantinople's main thoroughfares.

The separation of the Christian worshiping assembly by gender was a very common phenomenon until recently.

Procopius subordinates the human skill of the builders to the vision of God that inspired them. The intent of the building was to raise the minds of the worshipers to the contemplation of God. It is characteristic of Byzantine thought that, in spite of its immense size and magnificence, the church inspired a sense not of God's majesty but of God's nearness.

all. But I shall allow my readers to form a judgment by a single example. That part of the shrine which is especially sacred, where only priests may enter, which they call the Inner Sanctuary, is embellished with forty thousand pounds' weight of silver.

Source: The description of the newly built Hagia Sophia by Procopius can be found in *Procopius*, with an English translation by H. B. Dewing, with G. Downey, volume 7 of *Buildings*, Loeb Classical Library (Cambridge: Harvard University Press, 1940), pp. 13, 17-29. The Greek text from which Dewing translated is found on parallel pages. (This excerpt is reprinted by permission of the publishers and the Trustees of the Loeb Classical Library from *Procopius*, vol. 7, Loeb Classical Library, volume 343, translated by H. B. Dewing, with the collaboration of Glanville Downey, pp. 17-29. Cambridge, Mass.: Harvard University Press, copyright 1940 by the President and Fellows of Harvard College. Loeb Classical Library is a registered trademark of the President and Fellows of Harvard College.) Another translation of Procopius can be found in *The Art of the Byzantine Empire, 312-1453*, ed. Cyril Mango, Medieval Academy Reprints for Teaching, 16 (Toronto: University of Toronto Press, 1986).

Paul the Silentiary's Description of Hagia Sophia's Grandeur

Soon after the consecration of the rebuilt Hagia Sophia on December 24, 562, Byzantine poet Paul the Silentiary described the magnificence of the space in two long poems. As Paul's title shows, he was a member of the imperial court; silentiaries, whose original task was to insure that silence was kept in the emperor's presence, were often close confidants of the emperor. The first poem, the thousand-line "Description of the Holy Church," was recited before the emperor and the patriarch, probably either in the patriarchal palace or in the church, early in 563. Paul begins by describing the damage the church suffered in the earthquakes of 557, and continues by telling the story of the rebuilding. As scholar Cyril Mango has noted, "He goes on to describe how Justinian was roused to action; how he visited the ruins of the church and praised the skill of the architect Anthemius; how the church was rebuilt and re-consecrated."[1] Only then does the description proper of the church begin. The second poem of about three hundred lines is devoted to a description only of the ambo, the elevated platform in the center of the church from which the Bible was read. Although it is couched in poetic flourishes, Paul gives us the best eyewitness description of the original furnishings of the church, which are now lost.

Paul the Silentiary's "Description of the Holy Church"

. . . [186][2] Now the wondrous curve of the half-sphere, although resting on powerful foundations, collapsed and threw down the entire precinct of the sacred house. . . . [198] Yet, the broad-breasted fane [church] did not sink to the foundations, . . . but the curve of the eastern arch slipped off, and a portion of the dome was mingled with the dust: part of it lay on the floor, and part — a wonder to behold — hung in midair as if unsupported. . . .

[352] To the east there open the triple spaces of circles cut in half, and above, upon the upright collar of the walls, springs up the fourth part of a sphere: even so, above his triple-crested head and back does a peacock raise his many-eyed feathers. Men of the craft in their technical language call these crowning parts conches. . . . [362] The middle one is girded by the priestly seats and steps ranged in a circle: the lowest part of them is drawn close together round a center on the ground, but as they rise, they widen out little by little until they reach the stalls of silver, and so in ever-increasing circles they wheel round the curved wall that stands above them. This conch is followed by an arch resting on strong foundations, rectangular in plan and curved at the top, not in the form of a sphere, but in that of a cylinder cleft in twain; two other columned conches, one on each side, extend westward like bent arms stretched out to embrace within these mansions the band of singers. These conches

Paul describes the **synthronon**, the seats for the clergy in the eastern apse of the church.

1. Cyril Mango, from his introduction to the text in *The Art of the Byzantine Empire, 312-1453*, Medieval Academy Reprints for Teaching, 16 (Toronto: University of Toronto Press, 1986), p. 81.
2. Line numbers from the poems are given in brackets.

are lightened by columns speckled with purple bloom, ranged in half circle, holding aloft on golden capitals an overwhelming burden — columns which were once produced by the sheer crags of Thebes on the Nile. Thus on either side are the bases of each arcade upheld on twin columns, and along the traces of the threefold conch skilled workmen did bend from below smaller arches cut in half, under whose springing the columns have set their capitals, bound with bronze, carved, overlaid with gold, driving away all fear. Upon the porphyry columns stand others from Thessaly, splendid flowers of verdant stone. Here are the fair galleries for the women, and they have the same form that may be seen below, except that they are adorned not with two columns, but with six Thessalian ones. One may wonder at the resolve of the man who upon two columns has bravely set thrice two, and has not hesitated to fix their bases over empty air. All the spaces between, the Thessalian columns he has fenced with stone closures upon which the women may lean and rest their laborious elbows.

[398] Thus, as you direct your gaze towards the eastern arches, you behold a never-ceasing wonder. And upon all of them, above this covering of many curves, there rises, as it were, another arch borne on air, spreading out its swelling fold, and it rises to the top, to that high rim upon whose back is planted the base of the divine headpiece of the center of the church. Thus the deep-bosomed conch springs up into the air: at the summit it rises single, while underneath it rests on triple folds; and through fivefold openings pierced in its back it provides sources of light, sheathed in thin glass, through which, brilliantly gleaming, enters rosy-ankled Dawn. . . .

[417] And towards the west one may see the same forms as towards the dawn, though there is a small difference. For there in the central space it is not drawn in a curved arc as it is at the eastern end, where the priests, learned in the art of sacrifice, preside on seats resplendent with an untold wealth of silver; at the west is a great, richly wrought portal, not a single one, but divided into three at the boundary of the temple.

[425] By the doors there stretches out a lengthy porch receiving those that enter beneath wide gates. It is as long as the wondrous church is broad; this space is called narthex by the Greeks. Here through the night there rises a melodious sound pleasing to the ears of Christ, giver of life, when the psalms of God-fearing David are sung with alternate voice by the sacred ministers. . . . [438] Into the porch there open wide seven holy gates inviting the people to enter; one of these is on the narrow face of the narthex facing south, and another on the northern wing; the rest on their groaning pivots are opened by the warden in the west wall, which marks the end of the church.

Whither am I driven? What wind, as upon the sea, has carried away my roaming speech? The center of the church, the most renowned place, has been neglected. Return, my song, to behold a wonder scarcely to be believed when seen or heard.

[448] Next to the eastern and western circles — those circles cut in half — next to the twin Theban columns, are four sturdy piers, bare in front, but on their sides and powerful backs

Paul uses the sources of the marble to indicate color. Marble from Thebes was porphyry or purple; from Thessaly, green. The place names also indicate the distance from which the materials were brought and the great expense that went into the construction of the church.

Hagia Sophia's east-west orientation contributed to the splendor of its light. East-west axes were common in ancient churches and drew upon the course of the sun and symbolic associations with the Second Coming of Christ (cf. Matt. 24:27). Hagia Sophia excelled in the cumulative effect of numerous well-placed windows, and the luminescence of the building materials.

This reference to night-long singing of psalms is one of those frustratingly short hints of a practice about which historians would wish to know more.

they are bound by supports from opposite directions. The four of them rest on strong foundations, fixed on solid stones. In their midst the workman has mixed and poured the dust of fire-burnt stone, thus binding them together by the builder's art. Above them are bent arches of measureless size like the many-colored rounded bow of Iris: one turns towards the wing of Zephyr, another to Boreas, another to Notus; another rises upright towards fiery Eurus. Each arch joins its unshaken foot to that of the neighboring curve at either end, and so they are fixed together on the edge, but as each rises in the air in bending line, it slowly separates from its former fellow. Now, the space between the arches is filled with a fair construction. For where they bend away from one another according to the laws of art, and would have shown empty air, there springs up a wall in the shape of a triangle, sufficiently curved so as to join the arms on either side by the common yoke of a circular rim. On four sides these walls creep over and spread out, until they are united and run up on the back of the circle like a crown. The middle portion of the arches, as much as forms the curved rim, the builder's art has compacted of baked bricks, while the ends of the bows are made of construction stone. In the joints they have put sheets of soft lead lest the stones, pressing as they do upon one another and adding rude weight to weight, should have their backs broken; but with the lead inserted, the stone foundation is gently compressed.

[481] A stone rim, rounded on all sides, has been fastened upon the backs [of the arches], where the base of the hemisphere comes down; there, too, are the winding curves of the last circle which the workmen have set like a crown upon the backs of the arches. Under this projecting adornment suspended stones have fashioned a narrow path like a fringe upon which the lamplighter may fearlessly walk round and kindle the sacred lights.

[489] Rising above this into the immeasurable air is a helmet rounded on all sides like a sphere and, radiant as the heavens, it bestrides the roof of the church. At its very summit art has depicted a cross, protector of the city. It is a wonder to see how [the dome], wide below, gradually grows less at the top as it rises. It does not, however, form a sharp pinnacle, but is like the firmament which rests on air. . . .

[506] At the very navel the sign of the cross is depicted within a circle by means of minute mosaic so that the Savior of the whole world may for ever protect the church; while at the base of the half-sphere are fashioned forty arched windows through which the rays of fair-haired Dawn are channeled. . . .

[532] Now, towards the east and the west, you will see nothing beneath the arches: all is air. But towards the murmuring south wind and the rainless north there rises a mighty wall up to the chin of the rounded arch, and it is illuminated by twice four windows. This wall rests below on stone props, for, underneath it, six Haemonian columns, like the fresh green of the emerald, hold up a tireless sinewy juncture (it is there that the women have their seats). These in turn are heaved upon massive heads by four columns fixed immovable on the ground, glittering jewels of Thessalian marble graced with locks of golden hair. They separate

It is important to remember that in Greek Paul's description is a poem for the public praise of the church, full of flowery language and metaphor. Here Paul uses personifications of the four winds from Greek mythology instead of directions of the compass.

We depend upon such descriptions to know how the church was decorated and what the decoration meant to the worshipers. The mosaic cross was apparently a new feature in the renovated dome. The earlier writer Procopius (p. 68) says that "the whole ceiling is overlaid with pure gold."

Paul is speaking here of the galleries, or balconies, that run above the aisles along the north and south sides and over the narthex at the west end of the church.

the middle mansion of the glorious church from the lengthy aisle that lies alongside. Never were such columns, high-crested, blooming like a grove with bright flowers, cut from the land of Molossis.

[550] But in the midst of the aisle, too, Anthemius of many crafts, assisted by the wisdom of Isidorus (for both of them, serving the will of the industrious Emperor, have built this prodigious church), have set up four more columns, shorter in measure than their neighbors, but as bright with verdant bloom, being as they are from the same quarry. Their goodly feet are not planted in the ground all in a row: instead, they are set on the pavement in facing pairs, and upon their heads, a vault, wound on fourfold arches, supports the underside of the women's abode. Close by, in the direction of the north wind, is a door that leads the people to the pure founts that cleanse human life and drive away the grievous scars of sin [i.e., the baptistery, which was located in a separate building outside the main church].

[567] Following these four graceful Thessalian columns, on either side, namely towards dusk and dawn, pierced cylindrical vaults are poised on the divinely built walls along the length of the aisle and serve for passage. Towards the north wind they open into double doors, whereas towards the south, over against the doors, are well-wrought spaces like chambers. And again towards the day and night stand two other columns from the Haemus and two pillars with lofty crests from famous Proconnesus, set close to the doors. Towards the east there is but one door, while towards the abode of black night the people enter through a double portal.

[580] On the south you will find a long aisle altogether similar to the northern one, yet it has something in addition: for it contains a space separated by a wall, reserved for the Ausonian emperor on solemn festivals. Here my sceptered king, seated on his customary throne, lends his ear to [the reading of] the sacred books.

[586] And whoever mounts up will find that the women's aisles on either side are similar to those below; but the one that runs above the narthex, to the west, is not like the other two.

[590] Now on the western side of this divine church you will see a court encompassed by four aisles: one of these is joined to the narthex, while the others are open wide, and various paths lead to them. At the prized center of the wide court stands a spacious fountain, cleft from the Iasian peaks; from it a burbling stream of water, forced by a brazen pipe, leaps into the air — a stream that drives away all suffering, when the people, in the month of the golden vestments, at God's mystic feast, draw by night the unsullied waters in vessels. . . .

[605] Upon the carved stone wall curious designs glitter everywhere. These have been produced by the quarries of sea-girt Proconnesus. The joining of the cut marbles resembles the art of painting, for you may see the veins of the square and

The "women's abode" refers specifically to the balconies on the sides of the church. Whether women were restricted to the balconies is a matter of dispute. The sources also mention women on the ground floor. In general, however, men and women were separated in worship.

The reference to "golden **vestments**" (specialized ceremonial clothing) looks like a tantalizing clue about early Byzantine worship, but Paul is probably talking not about the clergy's vestments but about the clothing of the Roman governmental consuls. The only color for church vestments noted in tenth-century liturgical books from Constantinople is white. "God's mystic feast" is the feast of Epiphany (January 6), during which waters were blessed in commemoration of Christ's baptism.

octagonal stones meeting so as to form devices: connected in this way, the stones imitate the glories of painting.

And outside the divine church you may see everywhere, along its flanks and boundaries, many open courts. These have been fashioned with cunning skill about the holy building that it may appear bathed all 'round by the bright light of day.

[617] Yet who, even in the thundering strains of Homer, shall sing the marble meadows gathered upon the mighty walls and spreading pavement of the lofty church? Mining [tools of] toothed steel have cut these from the green flanks of Carystus and have cleft the speckled Phrygian stone, sometimes rosy mixed with white, sometimes gleaming with purple and silver flowers. There is a wealth of porphyry stone, too, besprinkled with little bright stars that had laden the riverboat on the broad Nile. You may see the bright green stone of Laconia and the glittering marble with wavy veins found in the deep gullies of the Iasian peaks, exhibiting slanting streaks of blood red and livid white; the pale yellow with swirling red from the Lydian headland; the glittering crocus-like golden stone which the Libyan sun, warming it with its golden light, has produced on the steep flanks of the Moorish hills; that of glittering black upon which the Celtic crags, deep in ice, have poured here and there an abundance of milk; the pale onyx with glint of precious metal; and that which the land of Atrax yields, not from some upland glen, but from the level plain: in parts vivid green not unlike emerald, in others of a darker green, almost blue. It has spots resembling snow next to flashes of black so that in one stone various beauties mingle.

[647] Before one comes to the glitter of cut mosaic, the mason, weaving together with his hands thin slabs of marble, has figured upon the walls connected arcs laden with fruit, baskets, and leaves, and has represented birds perched on boughs. The twining vine with shoots like golden ringlets winds its curving path and weaves a spiral chain of clusters. It projects gently forward so as to overshadow somewhat with its twisting wreaths the stone that is next to it. Such ornament surrounds the beauteous church. And above the high-crested columns, underneath the projecting stone edge, is deployed a tapestry of wavy acanthus, a wandering contexture of spiky points, all golden, full of grace. It encompasses marble shields — discs of porphyry glittering with a beauty that charms the heart.

[664] The hills of Proconnesus have gladly offered their back to the life-giving Queen to cover the entire floor, while the polish of Bosporus stone shimmers gently, black with an admixture of white.

[668] The roof is compacted of gilded tesserae from which a glittering stream of golden rays pours abundantly and strikes men's eyes with irresistible force. It is as if one were gazing at the midday sun in spring, when he gilds each mountaintop.

[673] Indeed, our emperor, who has gathered all manner of wealth from the whole earth, from barbarians and Ausonians alike, did not deem a stone adornment sufficient for this divine, immortal temple in which Rome has placed all its proud hopes of joy. He has not

It was not merely the size, scope, and materials of Hagia Sophia's architecture that created a sense of wonder. The worshiper must have felt surrounded by the most luxurious of decorations.

The poetic name for Italy is Ausonia, so the "Ausonians" are Romans. Constantinople was the capital of the Roman Empire, and its inhabitants thought of themselves as Romans.

spared, too, an abundant enrichment of silver. The ridge of Pangaeus and the cape of Sunium have opened all their silver veins, and many a treasure-house of our lords has yielded its stores.

[682] For as much of the great church by the eastern arch as was set apart for the blood-less sacrifice is bounded not with ivory or cut stone or bronze, but it is all fenced under a cover of silver. Not only upon the walls which separate the priest from the choir of singers has he set plates of naked silver, but the columns, too, six sets of twain in number, he has completely covered with the silver metal, and they send forth their rays far and wide. Upon them the tool wielded by a skilled hand has artfully hollowed out discs more pointed than a circle, within which it has engraved the figure of the immaculate God who, without seed, clothed himself in human form. Elsewhere it has carved the host of winged angels bowing down their necks, for they are unable to gaze upon the glory of God, though hidden under a veil of human form — He is still God, even if He has put on the flesh that removes sin. Elsewhere the sharp steel has fashioned those former heralds of God [the prophets] by whose words, before God had taken on flesh, the divine tidings of Christ's coming spread abroad. Nor has the artist forgotten the images of those who abandoned the mean labors of their life — the fishing basket and the net — and those evil cares in order to follow the command of the heavenly King, fishing even for men and, instead of casting for fish, spread out the nets of eternal life [the apostles]. And elsewhere art has depicted the Mother of Christ, the vessel of eternal life, whose holy womb did nourish its own Maker. And on the middle panels of the sacred screen which form a barrier 'round the sanctified priests, the carver's tool has incised one symbol that means many words, for it combines the names of the Empress and Emperor:[3] It is like a shield with a boss in whose middle part has been carved the sign of the cross. And the screen gives access to the priests through three doors. For on each side the workman's hand has made a small door.

[720] And above the all-pure table of gold rises into the ample air an indescribable tower, reared on fourfold arches of silver. It is borne aloft on silver columns on whose tops each of the four arches has planted its silver feet. And above the arches springs up a figure like a cone, yet it is not exactly a cone: for at the bottom its rim does not turn 'round in a circle, but has an eight-sided base, and from a broad plan it gradually creeps up to a sharp point, stretching out as it does so eight sides of silver. At the juncture of each to the other stand long backbones which seem to join their course with the triangular faces of the eight-sided form and rise to a single crest where the artist has placed the form of a cup. The lip of the cup bends over and assumes the shape of leaves, and in the midst of it has been placed a shining silver orb, and a cross surmounts it all. May it be propitious! Above the arches many a curve of acanthus twists 'round the lower part of the cone, while at the top, rising over the edge, it

The "choir of singers," literally "many-tongued crowd," probably refers not to a special choir but to the congregation in general.

Paul describes the space and furnishings associated with the Eucharist (the "bloodless sacrifice"). Several things should be noted: the amount of precious materials used in this area; the screen which separated the space; and the emphasis upon the divinity of Jesus Christ as the Incarnate God. The screen Paul mentions will develop into the formal iconostasis (icon stand), prominent in Eastern Orthodox churches today. In the sixth century, it was waist-high and did not obscure what was happening at the altar.

Paul describes the **ciborium** rising above the altar table. See the ciborium depicted in the icon of Basil (p. 36).

3. The "Empress" and "Emperor" of § 682 are Theodora and Justinian I, who, for all practical purposes, were co-rulers. See their portraits on p. 33.

terminates in upright points resembling the fragrant fruit of the fair-leaved pear tree, glittering with light. Now where the sides of the base are fitted to each other are fixed silver bowls, and in each bowl is set a candelabrum like a candle that burns not, expressing beauty rather than giving light; for these are fashioned all 'round of silver, brightly polished. Thus the candle flashes a silver ray, not the light of fire. And on columns of gold is raised the all-gold slab of the holy table, standing on gold foundations, and bright with the glitter of precious stones.

Paul describes the silk cloth, made of "the produce of the foreign worm," covering the altar table. Silk production was a relatively new industry in Constantinople. In 552, East Syrian monks, sent for this purpose by Justinian, smuggled silkworm eggs out of China, hiding them in their staffs. The East Syrian church of Persia had an active missionary presence in China.

[755] Whither am I carried? Whither tends my unbridled speech? Let my bold voice be restrained with silent lip lest I lay bare what the eyes are not permitted to see. But you priests, as the sacred laws command you, spread out with your hands the veil dipped in the purple dye of the Sidonian shell and cover the top of the table. Unfold the cover along its four sides and show to the countless crowd the gold and the bright designs of skillful handiwork. One side is adorned with Christ's venerable form. This has been fashioned not by artists' skillful hands plying the knife, nor by the needle driven through cloth, but by the web, the produce of the foreign worm, changing its colored threads of many shades. Upon the divine legs is a garment reflecting a golden glow under the rays of rosy-fingered Dawn, and a chiton, dyed purple by the Tyrian seashell, covers the right shoulder beneath its well-woven fabric; for at that point the upper garment has slipped down while, pulled up across the side, it envelops the left shoulder. The forearm and hand are thus laid bare. He seems to be stretching out the fingers of the right hand, as if preaching His immortal words, while in His left He holds the book of divine message — the book that tells what He, the Lord, accomplished with provident mind when His foot trod the earth. The whole robe shines with gold: for on it gold leaf has been wrapped 'round thread after the manner of a pipe or a reed, and so it projects above the lovely cloth, firmly bound with silken thread by sharp needles. On either side stand two of God's messengers: Paul, replete with divine wisdom, and the mighty doorkeeper of the gates of heaven who binds with both heavenly and earthly bonds [Peter]. One holds the book pregnant with holy ordinance, the other the form of the cross on a golden staff. And both the cunning web has clothed in robes woven of silver; while rising above their immortal heads a golden temple enfolds them with three noble arches fixed on four columns of gold. And on the hem of the veil shot with gold, art has figured the countless deeds of the Emperors, guardians of the city: here you may see hospitals for the sick, there sacred fanes [churches]. And elsewhere are displayed the miracles of heavenly Christ, a work suffused with beauty. And upon other veils you may see the monarchs joined together, here by the hand of Mary, the Mother of God, there by that of Christ, and all is adorned with the sheen of golden thread.

Christ's pose on the altar cloth, as Paul describes it, is like that of Christ on p. 34, a typical pose in such icons. The worshipers would have recognized the gesture as a blessing like the blessings given by the bishop. It would have reminded them that Christ is the true high priest of their worship.

[806] Thus is everything clothed in beauty; everything fills the eye with wonder. But no words are sufficient to describe the illumination in the evening: you might say that some nocturnal sun filled the majestic temple with light. For the deep wisdom of our Emperors has stretched from the projecting stone cornice, on whose back is planted the foot of the

temple's lofty dome, long twisted chains of beaten brass, linked in alternating curves by many hooks. From many points on a long course these fall together to the ground, but before they reach the floor, their lofty path is checked, and they form an even choir. And to each chain he has attached silver discs, suspended circle-wise in the air 'round the central confines of the church. Thus, descending from their lofty course, they float in a circle above the heads of men. The cunning craftsman has pierced the discs all over with his iron tool so that they may receive shafts of fire-wrought glass and provide pendent sources of light for men at night. Yet not from discs alone does the light shine at night, for in the [same] circle you will see, next to the discs, the shape of the lofty cross with many eyes upon it, and in its pierced back it holds luminous vessels. Thus hangs the circling choir of bright lights. You might say you were gazing on the effulgent stars of the heavenly Corona close to Arcturus and the head of Draco.

[834] Thus the evening light revolves 'round the temple, brightly shining. And in a smaller, inner circle you will find a second crown bearing lights along its rim, while in the very center another noble disc rises shining in the air, so that darkness is made to flee.

[839] By the aisles, too, next to the columns on either side, they have placed in sequence single lamps, one apart from the other, and they go through the whole length of the far stretching church. Beneath each they have placed a silver vessel resembling a balance pan, and in the center of this rests a cup of burning oil. There is not, however, one equal level for all the lamps, but you will see some high, some low, in lovely curves of light as they glitter step-wise on their aerial path, suspended from twisted chains. In this manner does the twin-pointed Hyas shine, fixed in the parted forehead of Taurus. One may also see ships of silver bearing a luminous freight; suspended, they sail through the bright air instead of the sea, fearing neither the south wind nor late-setting Bootes. And down on the floor you will see elegant beams running between two-horned [supports] of iron, upon which extends a row of lights, servitors of the temple, connected by straight rods of red color. Some of these are on the floor, where the elegant columns have set their bases, while others are above the capitals, following the long path of the walls.

[862] Neither has the base of the deep-bosomed dome been left without light, for along the projecting stone of the curved cornice the priest has lit single lamps attached to bronze stakes. Just as a king, cherishing his virgin daughter, might place 'round her neck a lovely chain glowing like fire with rubies set in gold, so has our Emperor fixed 'round the cornice a revolving circle of lights that run along the whole base.

[871] There is also on the silver columns, above their capitals, a narrow path of access for the lamplighters, a path full of light, glittering with bright clusters; these one might compare to the mountain-reared pine tree or to the cypress of tender foliage. Pointed at the summit, they are ringed by circles that gradually widen down to the lowest curve that surrounds the base of the trunk; and upon them have grown fiery flowers. Instead of a root, bows of silver have been

affixed beneath these trees of flaming vegetation. And in the center of this beauteous grove, the form of the divine cross, studded with bright nails, blazes with light for mortal eyes.

[884] Countless other lights, hanging on twisted chains, does the church of ever-changing aspect contain within itself; some illumine the aisles, others the center or the east and west; others shed their bright flame at the summit. Thus the bright night smiles like the day and appears herself to be rosy-ankled. . . .

Paul the Silentiary's "Description of the Ambo"

In the absence of architectural evidence, we are left to conjecture from imprecise statements like this one exactly where the ambo was located.

. . . [50] In the center of the wide church, yet tending rather towards the east, is a kind of tower, fair to look upon, set apart as the abode of the sacred books. Upright it stands on steps, reached by two flights, one of which extends towards the night, the other towards the dawn. These are opposite to one another; but both lead to the same space that is curved like a circle; for here a single stone circumscribes a space that resembles a circle, but is not altogether equal to a complete curve, for it contracts a little and so draws out the outline of the stone. And towards the west and east the stone forms a neck projecting from the circle and resting upon the steps. Up to the height of a man's girdle our divine Emperor has erected beauteous walls, crescent-shaped, sheathed in silver. For he has not bent the silver right around the stone, but the silver slabs unfold into glorious curves in the middle and form a wall. The skillful craftsman has opened the curve sufficiently on either side so as to provide access to the flights of steps. Nor does fear seize those who descend the sacred steps because their sides are unfenced; for walls of shining marble have been artfully reared here, and they rise above the steps to such height as is needed to guide a man's hand. By grasping them, a man eases his toil as he mounts upwards. So, in a slanting line, these [parapets] rise on either side together with the steps that are between them and come to a stop.

[76] This stone, too, is not devoid of worth; for it was to some purpose that they quarried the wild summits of steep hills to have a far-stretching boundary of the long flights. The whole of it is adorned with skillful workmanship and glistens with the many hues of the natural stone. Its surface is covered, as it were, with eddying whirlpools, in places resembling an infinity of circles, while in others they stray from under the circles into winding curves. In parts is seen a rosy bloom mingled with pallor, or the fair brightness of human fingernails; in other places the brilliance turns to a soft white like the color of boxwood or the lovely semblance of beeswax which men wash in clear mountain streams and lay out to dry under the sun's rays: it turns silver-white, yet not completely altering its color, it shows traces of gold. So, too, does ivory, tinged by the passage of long years, turn its silvery color to quince-yellow. In places it has a dark sheen, yet marvelous Nature did not allow this livid color to spread, but has mixed cunning patterns into the stone, and a changeful silvery light flashes over it: sometimes it flows over a wide expanse tinged with the choicest hue of dark crocus-yellow;

sometimes it has a paler glow, like the light that creeps 'round the pointed horns of the new-born moon. Near a stony crag stands the sacred city [Hierapolis] which has given its famous name to this marble.

[105] That whole fair construction of stone, whence the precepts of divinely wise books are read out, has been artfully fixed on eight cunningly wrought columns. Two of these are towards the north, two towards the south wind, two towards the east, and two towards the abode of night. Thus [the structure] is heaved up, and underneath the stone there is, as it were, another chamber, wherein the sacred song is raised by fair children, heralds of wisdom. What is roof for those below is a floor for those above; the latter is like a spreading plain, made level for the feet of mortals, while the underside has been cut out and hollowed by the mason so that it rises from the sacred capitals, curving over with artful adornment, like the bent back of the hard-shelled tortoise or the oxhide shield which the agile warrior holds over his helmet when he leaps in the Pyrrhic dance. The rough face of this whole stone has been girded all round with silver, and upon it the skillful craftsman has traced with the point of his iron tool various trees and fair flowers, interspersed by the soft leaves of ivy, with its clusters and budding shoots.

[126] To provide an unshakable foundation for the entire [structure] — the steps, the floor, and the columns themselves — the skilled craftsman has raised underneath it a stone base, the height of a man's foot above the ground. And with a view to broadening this footing of the structure, they have placed on either side, 'round the belly in the middle, half-circles of stone, and the space that has been thus cut off they surrounded with separate columns erected in semicircular formation. Thus the whole belly is widened by means of four rich columns on either side, to north and to south, and the cavern is, like a house, protected on all sides by an encircling fence of stone. The lovely columns have been cut by the masons' strong picks in the Phrygian land, by the Mygdonian heights; and when a man beholds the bloom of the stone, he would say that white lilies have been mingled with rose cups and the soft petals of the short-lived anemone. In places the marble is rosy with a tinge of white; in others it is mostly white with a tinge of fiery red; here and there the veins are traversed by fine sinews and, mingling together, they flush with purple, like the blood of the Laconian shell.

[148] First then they laid 'round about, at the bottom, the cunningly wrought plinth resplendent with twisting curves, and upon it they firmly set up stone pedestals cut from the rich quarries of the Bosporus. They gleam white, but on their white skin a blue vein winds a scattered path. The mason has beautifully carved the eight sides of each pedestal, while the steel carving-tool has bound its round neck [with a collar] so that the column should rest securely upon the circular [top of] the pedestal that is affixed underneath. Throughout the space of the church shines the glory of each column set on its polished base, like a white cloud tinged by the ruddy rays of the sun rising above the horizon.

[163] In this manner was the half-circle ringed with four columns; and the other half was

The ambo from which the Scripture was read was elevated enough so that singers could stand underneath. The singers may have been literally children, since the top of the ambo may not have been high enough to accommodate adults underneath it. Because the ambo was out in the nave, among the people, several of the important acts of worship could be led from the midst of the congregation.

surrounded with another four columns, thus fashioning a fair mantle of stone 'round the well-wrought cavern. Observing that there were three intervals between the four columns, the skillful mason made a fence for them of marble from the Sacred City, right upon the plinth, and he gently curved this [fence of] fair stone. It was indeed proper that this crown of stone on the goodly floor of the undefiled fane should bear a sacred name. And in the outermost interval he inserted a stout door, slightly curved, through which the man entrusted with the holy books enters the precinct of the cave. Now the form of the cavern is identical both towards Garamas on the south and towards the Arimaspian wind as regards the columns, the plinth, and the fence. The doors, however, the workmen have not fixed in the same place, but one they have set westwards and the other eastwards — the western one to the north, while the southern door faces east. Moreover, the fence-walls do not stand to the same height as the columns, but they rise above the beauteous pavement as much as to hide the men in the depths of the cave. But the eight columns with their deeply carved capitals project above the fence-wall, even though both [columns and fence] are firmly planted upon one and the same level foundation plinth. The gilded capitals shine all 'round with a brilliant glow, like high peaks which the golden-rayed disc of the sun strikes with its arrows.

[191] And all the capitals that rise aloft are crowned above in circled order by an embracing rim of beams, which binds the columns together in one curve, though each is separate from the other. Fixed upon the rim you may see trees with fiery clusters, glittering afar with flowers of flame from their silver branches. Nor does each sapling shoot up at random, but it rises in the form of a regular cone with many loops covered with lights: starting with a wide circle, it gradually diminishes until it comes to a sharp point. And the fair girdle you see — the one that forms the rim — is colored on all sides with sapphire dust and crowned with golden ivy-leaves. Towards the home of Zephyr and towards fiery-winged Eurus, there are fixed upon the rim two silver crosses, one on each side, bent in the form of a shepherd's crook, upon which many a nail with curved head picks up the countless lights of the lamps.

[209] With such beauties is adorned the ambo of double access. It bears this name because it is ascended (ambatos) by holy paths, and here the people direct their attentive eyes as they listen to the immaculate mysteries of the divine word.

[213] And even for the steps they have used not ordinary cut stone, but one on whose white surface you may see thin veins of a beautiful deep-red color like true purple. Using unpolished stones, the mason has made rough the easy treads of the stairs, a secure support for the feet of men, lest anyone on the descending path slip down from above and fall unsteady to the floor. Thus, in orderly succession, one stone, as it rises above another, recedes from it, as much as to allow a man ascending to support his steps in turn.

[224] And as an island rises amidst the waves of the sea, adorned with cornfields, and vineyards, and blossoming meadows, and wooded heights, while the travelers who sail by are gladdened by it and are soothed of the anxieties and exertions of the sea; so in the midst of

Different churches have done various things in order to facilitate the hearing of Scripture in worship. In Hagia Sophia and other churches in Constantinople, the end was achieved by elevation and proximity to the people.

the boundless temple rises upright the tower-like ambo of stone adorned with its meadows of marble, wrought with the beauty of the craftsman's art. Yet, it does not stand altogether cut off in the central space, like a sea-girt island, but it rather resembles some wave-washed land, extended through the white-capped billows by an isthmus into the middle of the sea, and being joined fast at one point it cannot be seen as a true island. Projecting into the watery deep, it is still joined to the mainland coast by the isthmus, as by a cable.

[240] Such, then, is the aspect of this place; for, starting at the last step to the east, there extends a long strait until it comes near the silver doors and strikes with its lengthy plinth the sacred precinct. On either side it is bounded by walls. They have not used lofty slabs for this fence-wall, but of such a height as to reach the girdle of a man standing by. Here the priest who brings the good tidings passes along on his return from the ambo, holding aloft the golden book; and while the crowd strives in honor of the immaculate God to touch the sacred book with their lips and hands, the countless waves of the surging people break around. Thus, like an isthmus beaten by waves on either side, does this space stretch out, and it leads the priest who descends from the lofty crags of this vantage point to the shrine of the holy table. The entire path is fenced on both sides with the fresh green stone of Thessaly, whose abundant meadows delight the eye. And next to each Thessalian slab stands a post of equal height, yet in form not rounded like a cylinder. A man versed in figures would say that these posts had the shape of an elongated, as opposed to an equal-sided, cube. To join the Molossian slabs together, the masons have wedged one stone into another; and it is from the Phrygian hills that the stone-cutter has quarried these posts. When, to soothe your sorrows, you cast your eyes there, you might see snake-like coils twining over the fair marble, in beauteous wavy paths, there fiery red and white are set next to each other, and there is a color intermediate between the two, their lines bending in alternating coils, as they roll 'round on their convoluted path. And in other places you may see the natural markings of the stone that resemble in their changeful lines the moon and the stars. And on the upper rim of the fence-wall they have fixed another long stone produced by the same craggy hill, so that the Thessalian slabs, firmly fixed as they are on the foundations of the plinth below, should also be held at the top by another stone attachment, while their sides are bound together by the square posts, and so fixed immovable on the pavement. . . . [294] And at the eastern end, by the holy fence-walls of the altar, they have cut off the isthmus, so as to afford a speedier path to those who pass from side to side.

Such works as these has our bountiful Emperor built for God the King. . . .

Paul describes the solea, a walkway between the altar and the ambo. Barriers were necessary to keep the space clear so the ministers could take the Gospel book from the sanctuary to the ambo for the readings and back again.

Paul describes a practice of allowing the worshipers lining the sides of the solea to touch or kiss the Gospel book. Because Byzantine-rite churches no longer use an ambo like Hagia Sophia's, this procession of the Gospel is no longer practiced, though elements of it have been incorporated into what today is called "the little entrance."

The solea did not completely divide the church into two parts, but left room for movement from one side to the other.

Source: The description of the rebuilt Hagia Sophia by Paulus Silentiarius is the English translation of Cyril Mango in *The Art of the Byzantine Empire, 312-1453*, Medieval Academy Reprints for Teaching, 16 (Toronto: University of Toronto Press, 1986), pp. 80-96. (This excerpt from Mango, *The Art of the Byzantine Empire, 312-1453*, first edition, copyright 1972, pages 80-86, is reprinted by permission of Pearson Education, Inc., Upper Saddle River, N.J.) Mango bases his translation upon the edition of P. Friedländer, *Johannes von Gaza und Paulus Silentiarius* (Leipzig-Berlin, 1912).

ORDER OF SERVICE AND TEXTS

A Reconstruction of the Order of a Divine Liturgy of Saint Basil

The following is a hypothetical reconstruction of a Divine Liturgy celebrated in Hagia Sophia by the patriarch of Constantinople in the sixth century. It is impossible to describe with complete certainty what worship at the time would have been like, since all liturgical manuscripts date from a later period, and no detailed contemporaneous description seems to exist. What follows is not the translation of a worship service from a manuscript, but a conservative reconstruction by the present author utilizing the writings of Maximus Confessor (see p. 49) to provide the basic order, the earliest manuscript to provide the prayer texts, and the insights of current scholars on likely performance of the rite.[1] It is possible that other items were included in worship during that century. Many of the prayer texts are still in use, and the sources of their translations (when not by the present author) are given in the notes.

On their way to the church for the Sunday Divine Liturgy, the worshipers leave offerings of bread and wine at the skeuophylakion, a separate building located on the northeast corner of Hagia Sophia. Some of these offerings will be used for communion; others will be distributed to the poor. The worshipers gather in the western atrium and the other courtyards that surround the church to wait for the patriarch. The patriarch stops in the skeuophylakion to put on vestments. He takes some of the bread from the people's offerings, places it on a paten for use later in communion, and says the following prayer:

O God, our God, you sent the heavenly bread, the food for the whole world, our Lord and God Jesus Christ, as a savior and redeemer and benefactor, to bless and sanctify us. Bless this bread set forth and receive it on your heavenly altar. Out of your goodness and love for

The prayers of the liturgy show how the classic Trinitarian shape of worship was adapted to refute heresy. In the earliest period, prayer was addressed to God the Father through the mediation of Jesus Christ in the power of the Holy Spirit. Although these prayers are addressed to the Father, the concluding doxology (the giving of glory) is to all the persons of the Trinity. The change came about in the fourth century to show the equality of Father, Son, and Spirit, who are, to quote the Nicene Creed, "worshiped and glorified together."

---

1. This reconstruction owes much to — indeed, would not be possible without — the work of Juan Mateos and Robert F. Taft in the multi-volume *History of the Liturgy of St. John Chrysostom.* See especially the following volumes: Juan Mateos, *La célébration de la parole dans la liturgie Byzantine. Étude historique,* Orientalia Christiana Analecta 191 (Rome: Pontifical Oriental Institute, 1971); Robert F. Taft, *The Great Entrance: A History of the Transfer of the Gifts and Other Preanaphoral Rites of the Liturgy of St. John Chrysostom,* OCA 200 (Rome: Pontifical Oriental Institute, 1978); Taft, *The Diptychs,* OCA 238 (Rome: Pontifical Oriental Institute, 1991); Taft, *The Precommunion Rites,* OCA 261 (Rome: Pontifical Oriental Institute, 2000); and Taft, *The Communion, Thanksgiving, and Concluding Rites,* OCA 281 (Rome: Pontifical Oriental Institute, 2008). Although these volumes are focused on the history of the liturgy of St. John Chrysostom, they also contain invaluable information about the liturgy of Basil, the main Eucharistic liturgy of Constantinople in the sixth century. Also valuable have been the reconstructions of the sixth-century Eucharistic ritual by Thomas Mathews in *The Early Churches of Constantinople: Architecture and Liturgy* (University Park: Pennsylvania State University Press, 1971), chapters 6 and 7, and Hugh Wybrew, *The Orthodox Liturgy: The Development of the Eucharistic Liturgy in the Byzantine Rite* (Crestwood, N.Y.: St. Vladimir's Seminary Press, 1990).

humanity be mindful of those who have offered it and those for whom they have offered it, and keep us blameless in the ministry of your divine mysteries. For blessed and glorified is your all-holy and magnificent name, of the Father and the Son and the Holy Spirit, now and forever and unto the ages of ages. Amen.[2]

The patriarch then proceeds to the atrium, where the people are waiting for him. Entering the narthex, the patriarch says the following prayer. His view through the doors reveals the worship space bathed in the sunlight streaming through the eastern windows:[3]

O Sovereign Lord, our God, you have appointed the orders and armies of angels and archangels to serve your glory in heaven. Grant that with our entry here, there will be an entry of holy angels to serve and glorify your goodness with us. For to you are due all glory, honor, and worship, to the Father and to the Son and to the Holy Spirit, now and ever and unto ages of ages.

The patriarch and the entire church then enter the worship space together to the following sung psalm. There is a standard way for singing psalms in this period, largely lost in later development of the Byzantine rite. Chanters sing the psalm verses, and the people are responsible for the refrain, which at the beginning of the sixth century is a famous piece known as the Trisagion, an expansion of the hymn of the seraphim in Isaiah 6:3. The likely psalm is 95:1-6a.

Soloist:

Holy God, Holy Mighty, Holy Immortal, have mercy on us. *(Three times.)*

People:

Holy God, Holy Mighty, Holy Immortal, have mercy on us. *(Three times.)*

Soloist:

Come, let us sing for joy to the LORD; let us shout aloud to the Rock of our salvation.

People:

Holy Immortal, have mercy on us.

Soloist:

Let us come before him with thanksgiving and extol him with music and song.

Referring to armies of angels shows the hidden significance of worship. The architecture and space visually reinforce this truth. The prayer sets up a clear act of assembling by the church.

In Western Christian churches, the people gathered inside the church and waited for the worship leader to enter. In Constantinople the people gathered outside the church and waited for the worship leader to lead them inside. The gathering and entrance emphasized the unity of the people in worship.

Notice the use of Scripture for something other than just a reading. Psalm 95 here provides an exhortation to gather and interprets the significance of this act of worship.

---

2. Unless otherwise indicated, translations of prayers are by the present author from the earliest text of the liturgy of Basil, edited by Stefano Parenti and Elena Velkovska, *L'euchologio Barberini Gr. 336* (Rome: C.L.V. — Edizioni liturgiche, 1995), folios 1-2.

3. For this description of the space, see Robert F. Taft, "The Liturgy of the Great Church: An Initial Synthesis of Structure and Interpretation on the Eve of Iconoclasm," *Dumbarton Oaks Papers* 34/35 (1980-1981): 50.

People:

Holy Immortal, have mercy on us.

Soloist:

For the LORD is the great God, the great King above all gods.

People:

Holy Immortal, have mercy on us.

Soloist:

In his hand are the depths of the earth, and the mountain peaks belong to him.

People:

Holy Immortal, have mercy on us.

Soloist:

The sea is his, for he made it, and his hands formed the dry land.

People:

Holy Immortal, have mercy on us.

Soloist:

Come, let us bow down in worship.

People:

Holy Immortal, have mercy on us.

Soloist:

Glory to the Father and to the Son and to the Holy Spirit, now and forever and to the ages of ages.

People:

Holy Immortal, have mercy on us.

Soloist:

Holy God, Holy Mighty, Holy Immortal, have mercy on us.

A kind of ancient praise chorus (simple lyrics with multiple repetitions) provides the congregational reponse to the verses of the psalm. By using a chorus, the people can learn their part easily and be freed up for movement, two strengths of choruses. This particular chorus, an adaptation of Isaiah 6:3, the song of the seraphim, continues the theme of participation in angelic worship.

People:

Holy God, Holy Mighty, Holy Immortal, have mercy on us.[4]

In the sixth century, another refrain was introduced for this introit by the emperor Justinian I, who may also have been its author. This refrain is known as Ho Monogenes *(the Only-Begotten):*

Notice that this hymnic prayer has essential remembrance about what God has done to save us: Christ was born, died, and rose for us. This repetition of core Gospel truth is the basis for Christian praying of all sorts. This sixth-century hymn also addresses a main concern of non-Chalcedonian believers, that Christ was the eternal Word of God himself, one of the Trinity.

O only-begotten Son and Word of God, though you are immortal you consented for our salvation to become incarnate of the holy Theotokos and ever-virgin Mary; you were made human without change and then, O Christ God, you were crucified, subduing death by your death. As one of the Holy Trinity, you are glorified together with the Father and the Holy Spirit. Save us.[5]

On certain feast days the emperor meets the patriarch in the narthex, and they go into the church together. After the entrance procession, the Gospel book is placed on the altar table. If the emperor is there, he puts a gift of money on the altar and goes to his throne in the south aisle. The patriarch ascends to his throne in the apse at the eastern end of the church, then turns and greets the people: "Peace be unto all." The ascent of the bishop concludes the first major movement in the worship service, the gathering and entrance into the church.

Reading multiple Scriptures is the classic way to make the overall biblical story the mainstay of ancient worship content.

Readings follow from the Old Testament, a New Testament Epistle, and a Gospel. Between the readings, psalms are sung with congregational refrains in the manner suggested above. Here the refrains are verses from the psalms and, at the psalm before the Gospel reading, alleluias. Before the Gospel reading, the patriarch again greets the people with a declaration of peace. The Gospel book is carried from the sanctuary along the solea to the ambo, where the Bible readings take place, and then back again. On the way back to the sanctuary, the deacon lets the worshipers close to the solea kiss the book. This procession of the Gospel book is the second major movement in the service.

After the readings, a sermon is preached.

Following this ministry of the Word, the patriarch descends from his throne to the altar. The catechumens (non-baptized people) are dismissed. The descent of the bishop and the dismissal of the

---

4. For a description of psalm practices, see Robert F. Taft, *Beyond East and West: Problems in Liturgical Understanding,* 2nd ed. (Rome: Pontifical Oriental Institute, 2001), pp. 196-99, 216-17. For the likely psalm, see Taft, *The Byzantine Rite: A Short History* (Collegeville, Minn.: The Liturgical Press, 1992), p. 37. For the discussion of the Trisagion and the Ho Monogenes, see Taft, *The Byzantine Rite,* p. 37; Taft, "The Liturgy of the Great Church," p. 50; Hugh Wybrew, *The Orthodox Liturgy,* pp. 77-78; and Hans-Joachim Schulz, *The Byzantine Liturgy,* trans. Matthew J. O'Connell (New York: Pueblo Publishing Co., 1986), pp. 24, 30.

5. This text can be found in F. E. Brightman, *Liturgies: Eastern and Western* (Oxford: Clarendon Press, 1896; reprint ed., 1965), pp. 365-66.

catechumens constitute the third major movement of the liturgy as the congregation is reconfig-ured for the communion service. There is a solemn closing of the doors after the dismissal.

The first act of this baptized assembly is a major intercessory prayer known as a litany. A dea-con leads it, and the people respond with a recurring petition. As the deacon asks the people to pray for a wide range of subjects (salvation, the world, Christian unity, clergy, lay faithful, government officials, the city and region, good weather and farming, travelers, the sick and the suffering, and deliverance from troubles), the people respond, "Lord, have mercy." The patri-arch, meanwhile, asks God to have mercy on those who are praying and then offers a conclud-ing petition:

You have given us grace to offer these common prayers in harmony. You have promised to grant the requests of two or three gathered in harmony in your name. Fulfill now the peti-tions of your servants for our benefit, giving us the knowledge of your truth in the present age and eternal life in the age to come. For you are good and you love humanity, and to you we give glory, to the Father and the Son and the Holy Spirit, now and ever and unto ages of ages. Amen.[6]

Following this intercessory prayer come several actions that lead toward Communion. Deacons bring the elements needed for the Eucharist from the skeuophylakion in a procession that winds its way through the north aisle, behind the ambo, and up the solea to the altar table. If the em-peror is present, he and his entourage join the procession behind the ambo, where he is given a candle to carry in front of the gifts. The emperor stops in front of the sanctuary barrier while the bread and wine are carried inside the sanctuary and deposited on the altar table. This procession with the communion elements is the fourth major movement of the service. While the deacons bring the Eucharistic elements, the people prepare themselves by singing the following refrain to Psalm 24:7-10:

Soloist:

Let us, who mystically represent the Cherubim, and who sing the Thrice-Holy Hymn to the Life-creating Trinity, lay aside all earthly cares, that we may receive the King of all, who comes invisibly escorted by the angelic hosts. Alleluia. *(Three times.)*

People:

Let us, who mystically represent the Cherubim, and who sing the Thrice-Holy Hymn to the

As a a greater percent-age of the population became Christian and infant baptism became the norm, the significance of the dismissal of catechu-mens declined.

Notice the location of the main interces-sory prayer (after the Word of God). Scripture readings — words from God to humans — dominate the first part of the service; prayer — words from humans to God — dominates the second. The use of a recurring phrase makes the people's participation easier.

The emperor's participation in pro-cessions highlights the incorporation of imperial ritual into the church's worship, showing both the importance and the limits of his role in the church. He leads the procession of the gifts through the place of the laity but stops outside the altar area, where the clergy receive the gifts.

---

6. This reconstruction follows the suggestion of Juan Mateos in *La célébration de la parole* (pp. 57-61): that two of the prayers accompanying the opening hymns in the eighth-century Byzantine liturgy earlier comprised Basil's Prayers of the Faithful. We reverse Mateos's suggested order of prayers, however.

Again, Scripture is used for something other than a reading. And, again, the people are given a praise chorus to make it easier for them to participate. The adoration expressed by the chorus makes it clear that we are dealing with something heavenly and significant in worship.

Life-creating Trinity, lay aside all earthly cares, that we may receive the King of all, who comes invisibly escorted by the angelic hosts. Alleluia. *(Three times.)*

Soloist:

Lift up your heads, O you gates; be lifted up, you ancient doors, that the King of glory may come in.

People:

Alleluia.

Soloist:

Who is he, this King of glory? The LORD strong and mighty, the LORD mighty in battle.

People:

Alleluia.

Soloist:

Lift up your heads, O you gates; be lifted up, you ancient doors, that the King of glory may come in.

People:

Alleluia.

Soloist:

Who is he, this King of glory? The LORD Almighty — he is the King of glory.

People:

Alleluia.

Soloist:

Glory to the Father and to the Son and to the Holy Spirit, now and forever and to the ages of ages.

People:

Alleluia.

Soloist:

Let us, who mystically represent the Cherubim, and who sing the Thrice-Holy Hymn to the

Life-creating Trinity, lay aside all earthly cares, that we may receive the King of all, who comes invisibly escorted by the angelic hosts. Alleluia.

People:

Let us, who mystically represent the Cherubim, and who sing the Thrice-Holy Hymn to the Life-creating Trinity, lay aside all earthly cares, that we may receive the King of all, who comes invisibly escorted by the angelic hosts. Alleluia.[7]

Meanwhile, the patriarch prepares for the Eucharist by washing his hands and asking prayers from his fellow ministers. He approaches close to the altar and says a prayer something like this:

O God, who in mercy and compassion has visited our lowliness, who has appointed us, your lowly, sinful, and unworthy servants, to minister at your holy altar, strengthen us for this ministry by the power of your Holy Spirit, so that, standing in the presence of your sacred majesty uncondemned, we may offer you a sacrifice of praise. For it is you alone who accomplish all things in all people. Grant, Lord, that our sacrifice may be acceptable and welcome in your presence, for our sins and the faults of the people.[8]

The kiss of peace is then exchanged, and all say the following creed:[9]

I believe in one God, the Father, the Almighty,

Creator of heaven and earth, and of all things visible and invisible.

And in one Lord, Jesus Christ, the only begotten Son of God,

begotten of the Father before all ages.

Light of Light, true God of true God, begotten, not created,

of one essence with the Father, through whom all things were made.

For us and for our salvation, He came down from heaven

and was incarnate by the Holy Spirit and the Virgin Mary and became man.

He was crucified for us under Pontius Pilate, and He suffered and was buried.

On the third day He rose according to the Scriptures.

He ascended into heaven and is seated at the right hand of the Father.

He will come again in glory to judge the living and the dead.

His kingdom will have no end.

The kiss of peace is not simply a "hello" but a significant gesture of the love and peace that the Lord gave after his Resurrection. In the early church, it was an actual kiss that the faithful exchanged. In sixth-century Constantinople, men exchanged it only with men, and women with women.

The creed, first introduced into the liturgy in the late fifth century, serves as a kind of summary for the whole content of faith and worship: the service is about the Triune God, who is active from the creation of the world to the return of Jesus Christ.

7. In *The Great Entrance*, pp. 116-17, Taft describes the execution of this refrain and psalm in the sixth century. This particular refrain, called the "Cherubic Hymn," was introduced in 573. The previous refrain was probably simply "Alleluia."

8. This reconstruction is based upon the current Prayers of the Faithful in the liturgy of Basil, following the translations and arguments of Taft in *The Great Entrance*, pp. 366-69. Taft's material is used by permission.

9. This translation is from the Greek Orthodox Archdiocese of America. It is used with permission.

The Western reader will notice that the phrase "and the son" is missing after "proceeds from the Father"; here the Holy Spirit only "proceeds from the Father." The phrase "and the son" (Latin: *filioque*) was not original to the creed but was first added in Spain in the seventh century. Its acceptance by the Roman church in the eleventh century was the final spark igniting the schism between East and West that continues to this day.

And in the Holy Spirit, the Lord, the Giver of Life,

who proceeds from the Father,

who together with the Father and the Son is worshiped and glorified,

who spoke through the prophets.

In one, holy, catholic, and apostolic Church.

I acknowledge one baptism for the forgiveness of sins.

I expect the resurrection of the dead.

And the life of the age to come. Amen.

The patriarch then prays the Eucharistic prayer, known as an anaphora. It is likely that most of the prayer is said in a low voice unheard by the people. In this early period, the Eucharistic prayer ascribed to St. Basil the Great (4th c., Cappadocia) is the main text used. On some occasions, it is the Anaphora of St. John Chrysostom (4th c., from Antioch; archbishop of Constantinople, 398-407) that is used. At a later date, the Chrysostom Anaphora will become the predominant prayer said. Translations of both prayers are provided (see pp. 93-99 and pp. 100-103). Maximus the Confessor notes that the people join in the angelic acclamation ("Holy, Holy, Holy," and so on) within the anaphora.

Ecumenical councils, in this volume, are used to mean one of a series of general councils where bishops from the whole church met to discuss and settle matters of church doctrine. The diptychs were lists of living and dead members of the church to be remembered in prayer.

*During the anaphora, deacons lead the congregation in special commemorations, reading the **diptychs**, which remember notable dead (patriarchs, bishops, fathers of **ecumenical councils**, other clergy, sovereigns, and all deceased Orthodox Christians) and living members of the church. Because inclusion on these lists indicates a state of recognition or fellowship with those named, these lists were sometimes vehicles of political struggle in tumultuous theological and political times.*

Following the anaphora there is a short litany, which concludes with the following prayer. This is the ancient prayer of preparation for communion, which retained its character even after the Lord's Prayer was inserted into the liturgy in the fourth century:

Our God, the God who saves, teach us to thank you worthily for the good things that you have done and still do for us. You are our God and have accepted these gifts. Cleanse us from every defilement of flesh and spirit, and teach us how to perfect holiness in your fear, so that, receiving the portion of your holy gifts with a clear conscience, we may be united with the holy Body and Blood of your Christ. Having received them worthily, may we have Christ dwelling in our hearts, and may we become the temple of your Spirit. Let none of us be guilty of these, your awesome and heavenly mysteries, O God, nor be infirm in body and soul by partaking of them unworthily. But enable us, even up to our last breath, to receive the hope of your holy gifts worthily, as provision for eternal life and as an acceptable defense at the awesome judgment seat of your Christ, so that we also, together with all the saints who through the ages have pleased you, may become partakers of your eternal good things, which you, Lord, have prepared for those who love you.

The whole church then joins in the Lord's Prayer:

Our Father in heaven, hallowed be your name. Your kingdom come,
your will be done, on earth as it is in heaven. Give us this day our daily bread,
and forgive us our trespasses, as we forgive those who trespass against us.
And lead us not into temptation, but deliver us from evil.
For yours is the Kingdom and the power and the glory of the Father and of the Son
and of the Holy Spirit, now and ever and unto ages of ages. Amen.

After the Lord's Prayer, the patriarch greets the people. Certain people who are in the last stage of a process of public penance for grievous sin — who are permitted to pray with the faithful but not receive communion — are dismissed from the assembly with prayer.[10] The patriarch then invites the remaining faithful to communion:

Patriarch:
The holy gifts for holy people.

People:
One is holy. One is the Lord: Jesus Christ, to the glory of God the Father. Amen.

Communion follows. People process to the front of the church to receive communion at small, portable tables that are set up outside the barrier around the altar to hold the plates of communion bread and chalices of wine. The people receive the bread in their hands, while ministers hold chalices for them to drink from, as can be seen in the engraving on the sixth-century Riha paten (p. 29). The procession to receive communion constitutes the fifth major movement in the service. During communion, which can take an hour or more to complete, Psalm 148 is sung several times as the people interject alleluias between the verses in the manner illustrated above. Other psalms are used on other occasions.

This service uses a few standard elements that will occur in every service. That helps the congregation feel familiar with the service even while some elements change from week to week. The use of the Lord's Prayer as preparation for Communion is common from the fourth century on.

In the early church, baptized people were sometimes excluded from the church assembly for serious public sins, including murder, adultery, and apostasy (renunciation of their Christian faith). Public penance was a way of gradually letting those who publicly repented of their sins back into the assembly. In the last stage of this process, penitents were allowed to attend the communion service but not receive communion.

10. After the practice of public penance ceased, this dismissal of penitents became a general prayer said over the whole congregation as they bowed their heads; see Taft, *Precommunion Rites*, pp. 173-97. Taft does not suggest a precise date for this change. That it had not yet taken place by the sixth century is suggested by evidence that public penance was still in force then (see Taft, *Precommunion Rites*, pp. 181-82) and the fact that Maximus the Confessor does not mention a bowing of the heads at this point in his *Mystagogy*, as he might have had it pertained to all the faithful.

Following communion, the patriarch says a prayer of thanksgiving to God for the communion received.

A dismissal concludes the service:

Deacon:
Let us go forth in peace.

People:
In the name of the Lord.

As the clergy recess out of the space, the patriarch stops one last time near the ambo (the raised platform for readings) and prays the following:

> O Lord our God, save your people and bless your inheritance. Protect the whole body of your church, and sanctify those who love the beauty of your house. Glorify them in return by your divine power, and do not forsake us who hope in you. Give peace to your world, to the churches, to the priests, to our emperor and empress, and to all your people. For holy is your temple, wonderful in righteousness, and we send up glory to you, to the Father and to the Son and to the Holy Spirit, now and forever and unto the ages of ages. Amen.[11]

The clergy carry the chalices used for the wine and the plates used for the bread back to the skeuophylakion, where the patriarch says a final prayer reflecting on the service they have just celebrated:

> All the customary mysteries of incorruption have been accomplished and completed insofar as we are able. We have had a memorial of your death, we have seen a figure of your resurrection, we have been filled with your inexhaustible food, we have enjoyed your unending life. Grant that we may obtain this unending life also in the age to come, O Christ our God. For you are worthy of all thanksgiving, with your Father without beginning and your all-holy, good, and life-creating Spirit, now and ever, and unto the ages of ages. Amen.[12]

Notice that the patriarch, the one responsible for Word and sacrament, also does the concluding act of worship. The roles are clear among the various kinds of worship leaders. The recession of the clergy and the dispersal of the people constitute the sixth and final major movement of the worship service.

This prayer captures the Byzantine understanding of the liturgical "mystery." In the performance of the mysteries — the liturgical symbols — we already enjoy eternal life, even though its fulfillment awaits the age to come. The liturgy is the experience now of the future age: a taste of heaven on earth.

---

11. See Mathews, *The Early Churches of Constantinople*, p. 173, and Taft, *The Communion, Thanksgiving, and Concluding Rites*, pp. 583-88, for when the prayer was said. In his book, Taft suggests (pp. 598-602) that the prayer was recited from the back of the ambo itself.

12. In *The Communion, Thanksgiving, and Concluding Rites* (pp. 609-10), Taft is certainly correct that this prayer and the previous prayer are later additions to the liturgy, since they come after the dismissal proper. But as he also argues, the names these prayers are given in the later manuscripts — "behind the ambo," "of the skeuophylakion" — show that they entered the liturgy before the rearrangement of the church furnishings that followed Iconoclasm (c. 730-843). Whether they had already entered the liturgy by the sixth century is impossible to say. Nevertheless, as Taft also notes, these prayers provide an elegant balance in the liturgy, which begins and ends with prayer in the skeuophylakion and features prayer while entering the church and prayer while leaving the church (*The Communion, Thanksgiving, and Concluding Rites,* pp. 588-91). These prayers make optimal use of the liturgical space.

The Main Prayer of Consecration Said at the Lord's Supper in the Sixth Century

Byzantine worship uses two different liturgies for the Lord's Supper. Named after influential fourth-century theologians, one of these is known as the Liturgy of Basil of Caesarea (Cappadocia), the other as the Liturgy of John Chrysostom. They differ in their prayers and, in particular, in the central Prayer of Thanksgiving said over the bread and wine for communion, the Eucharistic prayer or anaphora. The Eucharistic prayer is often called the prayer of consecration because through it the bread and the wine are consecrated for communion. But its first function in all early liturgies was to respond to the command "Let us give thanks to the Lord." Thanksgiving (in Greek, eucharistia*) is the central action of the whole service and gives it its name, Eucharist. Both Byzantine anaphoras are thanksgivings that honor God by reciting salvation history, culminating with statements of offering, petitions for the Holy Spirit to come, and prayers of intercession. They tell the story of salvation in different ways, however, using different Bible verses. Basil's anaphora uses Hebrews 1:1-12 to focus on Christ's revelation to us of God the Father. The anaphora also has a developed Trinitarian theology, again centering on Christ's role of manifesting the Father and revealing the Spirit.*

Below is the anaphora of the main liturgy used in the sixth century, that of Basil, translated by R. C. D. Jasper and G. J. Cuming from the oldest Greek manuscript, Barberini Gr. 336 in the Vatican Library, from the eighth century, supplemented at a gap by the ninth- or tenth-century Grottaferrata MS G b vii. Material from later manuscripts and printed editions not found in these early manuscripts, including the people's parts, has been put in angle brackets (⟨ ⟩), while material from the early manuscripts not found in later versions has been put in square brackets ([ ]).

Priest:

The grace of our Lord Jesus Christ and the love of the God and Father and the fellowship of the Holy Spirit be with you all.

People:

And with your spirit.

Priest:

Let us lift up our hearts.

People:

We have them with the Lord.

Scholars differ about whether and how either prayer was the direct work of the men whose names they bear, though some influence of these men is likely.

Material found only in later manuscripts was not necessarily unknown in the eighth or even the sixth century. These prayers, like the whole order of worship, are "living literature," which keeps a recognizable shape but varies according to the needs of the local church where and when the manuscripts were written.

"Priest" is an accurate translation of the word used in the eighth-century manuscript. In the context of sixth-century Constantinople, we should read "patriarch" or "bishop."

Some form of this dialogue of blessing between presider and people has been a standard feature of nearly all consecratory prayers across worship history.

Priest:

Let us give thanks to the Lord.

People:

It is fitting and right ⟨to worship the Father, the Son, and the Holy Spirit, the consubstantial and undivided Trinity⟩.

And the priest begins the holy anaphora:

I AM, Master, Lord God, Father almighty, reverend, it is truly fitting and right and befitting the magnificence of your holiness to praise you, to hymn you, to bless you, to worship you, to give you thanks, to glorify you, the only truly existing God, and to offer to you with a contrite heart and a humble spirit this our reasonable service. For it is you who granted us the knowledge of your truth; and who is sufficient to declare your powers, to make all your praises to be heard, or to declare all your wonders at all times? [Master,] Master of all, Lord of heaven and earth and all Creation, visible and invisible, you sit on the throne of glory and behold the depths, without beginning, invisible, incomprehensible, infinite, unchangeable, the Father of our Lord Jesus Christ, the great God and savior of our hope, who is the image of your goodness, the identical seal, manifesting you the Father in himself, living Word, true God, before all ages wisdom, life, sanctification, power, true Light by whom the Holy Spirit was revealed, the spirit of truth, the grace of sonship, the pledge of the inheritance to come, the firstfruits of eternal good things, life-giving power, the fountain of sanctification, by whose enabling the whole rational and spiritual Creation does you service and renders you the unending doxology; for all things are your servants. For angels, archangels, thrones, dominions, principalities, powers, virtues, and the cherubim with many eyes praise you, the seraphim stand around you, each having six wings, and with two covering their own faces, and with two their feet, and with two flying, and crying one to the other with unwearying mouths and never-silent doxologies, *(aloud)* singing the triumphal hymn, crying aloud and saying:

People:

Holy, ⟨holy, holy, Lord of **Sabaoth**; heaven and earth are full of your glory. Hosanna in the highest. Blessed is he who comes in the name of the Lord. Hosanna in the highest.⟩

The priest says privately:

With these blessed powers, Master, lover of men, we sinners also cry and say: you are truly holy and all-holy, and there is no measure of the magnificence of your holiness, and you are holy in all your works, for in righteousness and true judgment you brought all things upon us. For you took dust from the earth and formed man; you honored him with your image, O God, and set him in the paradise of pleasure, and promised him immortality of life

Among the contributions to the anaphora perhaps made by Basil himself in the fourth century is the reworking of the opening praise to include the Holy Spirit. This inclusion highlights the relationships of the Persons of the Trinity and rightly shows the Trinitarian character of classic Christian worship.

Sabaoth is a Hebrew word that means "hosts" or "armies," referring to angelic hosts. This prayer anticipates that through this act of praise the people would be participating in the angelic worship.

and enjoyment of eternal good things in keeping your commandments. But when he had disobeyed you, the true God who created him, and had been led astray by the deceit of the serpent, and had been subjected to death by his own transgressions, you, O God, expelled him in your righteous judgment from paradise into this world, and turned him back to the earth from which he was taken, dispensing to him the salvation by rebirth which is in your Christ. For you did not turn away finally from your creature, O good one, nor forget the works of your hands, but you visited him in many ways through the bowels of your mercy. You sent forth prophets; you performed works of power through your saints who were pleasing to you in every generation; you spoke to us through the mouth of your servants the prophets, foretelling to us the salvation that should come; you gave the Law for our help; you set angels as guards over us.

The term *man* can also be translated "humanity." The story of Adam is the story of humanity in general. Notice the shift to first-person "us" by the end of this paragraph.

But when the fullness of the times had come, you spoke to us in your Son himself, through whom also you made the ages, who, being the reflection of your glory and the impress of your substance, and bearing all things by the word of his power, thought it not robbery to be equal with you, the God and Father, but he who was God before the ages was seen on earth and lived among men; he was made flesh from a holy virgin and humbled himself, taking the form of a slave; he was conformed to the body of our humiliation that he might conform us to the image of his glory. For since through man sin had entered into the world, and through sin, death, your only-begotten Son, who is in your bosom, O God and Father, being born of a woman, the Holy Mother of God and ever-Virgin Mary, born under the law, was pleased to condemn sin in his flesh, that those who died in Adam should be made alive in him, your Christ. And having become a citizen of this world, he gave us commandments of salvation, turned us away from the error of the idols, and brought us to the knowledge of you, the true God and Father; he gained us for himself, a peculiar people, a royal priesthood, a holy nation; and when he had cleansed us with water and sanctified us by the Holy Spirit, he gave himself as a ransom to death, by which we were held, having been sold under sin. By means of the cross he descended into hell, that he might fill all things with himself, and loosed the pains of death; he rose again on the third day, making a way to resurrection from the dead for all flesh, because it was not possible for the prince of life to be conquered by corruption, and became the firstfruits of those who had fallen asleep, the firstborn from the dead, so that he might be first in all ways among all things. And ascending into the heavens, he sat down at the right hand of the majesty in the highest, and will also come to reward each man according to his works. And he left us memorials of his saving passion, these things which we have set forth according[1] to his commandments.

This prayer is carried along by vibrant verbs that commemorate God's activity. The prayer reflected an ancient sensibility that God is worshiped rightly by remembering God's activity. Notice that salvation history is interpreted with Christ as the key.

For when he was about to go out to his voluntary and laudable and life-giving death, in the night in which he gave himself up for the life of the world, he took bread in his holy and

---

1. The earliest surviving manuscript of this prayer, the eighth-century Barberini Gr. 336, breaks off here. The translation continues using the ninth- or tenth-century Grottaferrata MS G b vii.

The commemoration of Christ's institution of the Lord's Supper (known as the Words of Institution) is part of the prayer, not a separate exhortation addressed to the congregation.

undefiled hands and showed it to you, the God and Father, gave thanks, blessed, sanctified, and broke it, and gave it to his holy disciples and apostles, saying, "Take, eat; this is my body, which is broken for you for the forgiveness of sins."

People:

Amen.

Priest:

Likewise also he took the cup of the fruit of the vine and mixed it, gave thanks, blessed, sanctified, and gave it to his holy disciples and apostles, saying, "Drink from this, all of you; this is my blood, which is shed for you and for many for the forgiveness of sins."

People:

Amen.

Priest:

"Do this for my remembrance. For as often as you eat this bread and drink this cup, you proclaim my death, you confess my resurrection."

Therefore, Master, we also, remembering his saving Passion, his life-giving cross, his three-day burial, his resurrection from the dead, his ascension into heaven, his session at your right hand, God and Father, and his glorious and fearful second coming; *(aloud)* offer[ing] you your own from your own, in all and through all,

The people's refrain may have originated in Constantinople or in Basil's native Cappadocia. See the Anaphora of St. John Chrysostom (p. 102).

People:

we hymn you, ⟨we bless you, we give you thanks, O Lord, and pray to you, our God.⟩

Priest:

The word translated "make" in this prayer of consecration (line 7) is better translated as "show." It may represent an earlier theory of consecration in which the bread and wine are revealed to be the Body and Blood of Christ. The similar petition in the Anaphora of John Chrysostom asks that the bread and wine be "changed."

Therefore, Master all-holy, we also, your sinful and unworthy servants, who have been held worthy to minister at your holy altar, not for our righteousness, for we have done nothing good upon earth, but for your mercies and compassions which you have poured out richly upon us, with confidence approach your holy altar. And having set forth the likenesses of the holy body and blood of your Christ, we pray and beseech you, O holy of holies, in the good pleasure of your bounty, that your [all-]Holy Spirit may come upon us and upon these gifts set forth, and bless them and sanctify and *[he signs the holy gifts with the cross three times]* make this bread the precious body of our Lord and God and Savior Jesus Christ. Amen. And this cup the precious blood of our Lord and God and Savior Jesus Christ, [Amen.] which is shed for the life of the world ⟨and salvation⟩. Amen.

Unite with one another all of us who partake of the one bread and the cup into fellowship with the one Holy Spirit; and make none of us to partake of the holy body and blood of your Christ for judgment or for condemnation, but that we may find mercy and grace with all the saints who have been well-pleasing to you from of old, forefathers, fathers, patriarchs, prophets, apostles, preachers, evangelists, martyrs, confessors, teachers, and every righteous spirit perfected in faith; *(aloud)* especially our all-holy, immaculate, highly blessed ⟨glorious⟩ Lady, Mother of God and ever-Virgin Mary;

While the diptychs are read by the deacon, the priest continues the prayer:

Saint John the ⟨prophet,⟩ forerunner and Baptist, ⟨the holy and honored apostles,⟩ this saint *N.* whose memorial we are keeping, and all your saints: at their entreaties, visit us, O God.

And remember all those who have fallen asleep in hope of resurrection to eternal life, and grant them rest where the light of your countenance looks upon them.

Again we pray you, Lord, remember your holy, catholic, and apostolic church from one end of the world to the other, and grant it the peace which you purchased by the precious blood of your Christ, and establish this holy house until the consummation of the age, and grant it peace.

Remember, Lord, those who presented these gifts, and those for whom, and through whom, and on account of whom they presented them.

Remember, Lord, those who bring forth fruit and do good work in your holy churches, and remember the poor. Reward them with rich and heavenly gifts. Grant them heavenly things for earthly, eternal things for temporal, incorruptible things for corruptible.

Remember, Lord, those in deserts and mountains and in dens and in caves of the earth.

Remember, Lord, those who live in virginity and piety ⟨and self-discipline⟩ and an honest way of life.

Remember, Lord, our most religious and faithful Emperor, whom you thought fit to rule the land: crown him with the weapon of truth, with the weapon of your good pleasure; overshadow his head in the day of war; strengthen his arm, exalt his right hand; make his empire mighty; subject to him all the barbarous people that delight in war; grant him help and peace that cannot be taken away; speak good things to his heart for your church and all your people, that in his peace we may lead a quiet and peaceful life in all godliness and honesty.

Remember, Lord, all rule and authority, our brothers at court and all the army; preserve the good in their goodness; make the wicked good in your bounty.

Remember, Lord, the people who stand around and those who for good reason are absent, and have mercy on them and on us according to the abundance of your mercy. Fill their storehouses with all good things, preserve their marriages in peace and concord; nourish the infants, instruct the youth, strengthen the old; comfort the fainthearted, gather the scattered, bring back the wanderers and join them to your holy, catholic, and apostolic church; set free

---

Communion's goal is unity with God and one another. The list of saints emphasizes the unity between those on earth and those in heaven, as do the diptychs, the lists of names of those both living and dead, who are remembered by the community. While the text does not specify this, we assume that the priest would have continued the prayer in a low voice while the deacon read the diptychs aloud.

The petition for "those in deserts and mountains and in dens and in caves of the earth" quotes Hebrews 11:38. In the circumstances of the fourth-century church and later, it especially remembered monks and nuns, those Christians who had chosen to separate themselves to live a life of solitude and prayer, as sometimes in the caves of Basil's native Cappadocia.

This prayer for the emperor represents one of the ways Christians tried to work out the relationship of the emperor to the church after the conversion of Constantine. One of the tasks of the emperor was to preserve peace so that the church could flourish.

those who are troubled by unclean spirits; sail with those that sail, journey with those that journey; defend the widows, protect the orphans, rescue the captives, heal the sick. Be mindful, O God, of those who face trial, those in the mines, in exile, in bitter slavery, in all tribulation, necessity, and affliction; of all who need your great compassion, those who love us, those who hate us, and those who commanded us, though unworthy, to pray for them.

Remember all your people, O Lord our God, and pour out upon all your rich mercy, granting to all their petitions for salvation. Be mindful yourself of those whom we have not mentioned through ignorance or forgetfulness or the number of the names; O God, you know the age and the title of each, you know every man from his mother's womb. For you, Lord, are the help of the helpless, the hope of the hopeless, the savior of the tempest-tossed, the haven of sailors, the physician of the sick: yourself be all things to all men, for you know every man and his petition, his house, and his need.

Rescue, Lord, this flock, and every city and country, from famine, plague, earthquake, flood, fire, the sword, invasion by foreigners, and civil war.

⟨*aloud*⟩ Above all, remember, Lord, our Father and bishop *N.:* grant him to your holy churches in peace, safety, honor, health, and length of days, rightly dividing the word of your truth.

The diptychs of the living are read.

Deacon:

N. the all-holiest metropolitan (or bishop), and him who presents these holy gifts . . . and all men and women.

People:

And all men and women.

Priest:

Remember, Lord, all the orthodox episcopate who rightly divide the word of your truth.

Remember, Lord, also my unworthiness, according to the multitude of your mercies: forgive me the offense, willing and unwilling; and do not keep back, on account of my sins, the grace of your Holy Spirit from the gifts set forth.

Remember, Lord, the priesthood, the diaconate in Christ, and every order of the clergy, and do not put to shame any of us who stand 'round your holy altar.

Look upon us, Lord, in your goodness; appear to us in your rich mercies; grant us temperate and favorable weather; give kindly showers to the land for bearing fruit; bless the crown of the year of your goodness, Lord. End the divisions of the churches; quench the ragings of the nations; quickly destroy the uprising of heresies by the power of your Holy Spirit. Receive

The words rendered as "man" or "men" are better translated as "person" or "people." No discrimination is intended in the text.

The diptychs of the living included the heads of the other major churches — e.g., Rome, Alexandria, Antioch, and Jerusalem — with whom the Church of Constantinople was in communion. Remembering the heads of other churches in prayer was a witness to the unity of the church throughout the world.

Notice the breadth of the intercessions placed at the end of the consecratory prayer. The prayers here and elsewhere matched the scope of Christ's lordship.

us all into your kingdom, making us sons of light and sons of the day; grant us your peace and your love, Lord our God, for you have given us all things; *(aloud)* and grant us with one mouth and one heart to glorify and hymn your all-honorable and magnificent name, the Father and the Son and the Holy Spirit, now ⟨and always and to the ages of ages.⟩

People:

Amen.

The frequent use of instructions such as "aloud" and "privately" in the ninth-century text from which these prayers were translated shows that by then most of the Eucharistic prayer was said silently. In the sixth century there was a disagreement about whether this prayer should be said loud enough so that the people could hear it. (See p. 134.)

Source: The Liturgy of Basil of Caesarea is available in Greek in F. E. Brightman, *Liturgies: Eastern and Western* (Oxford: Clarendon Press, 1896; reprint ed., 1965), pp. 309-44. Brightman bases much of his text on the earliest surviving manuscript of these liturgies, Barberini Gr. 336 (8th century), which can be found in a critical edition titled *L'eucologio Barberini Gr. 336,* ed. Stefano Parenti and Elena Velkovska (Rome: C.L.V. — Edizioni Liturgiche, 1995). Brightman's edition of the gaps in the Barberini manuscript is supplied from Grottaferrata MS G b vii from the ninth or tenth century. The English translation of the anaphora of Basil reproduced here is from *Prayers of the Eucharist: Early and Reformed,* 3rd ed., ed. R. C. D. Jasper and G. J. Cuming (Collegeville, Minn.: The Liturgical Press, 1992), pp. 116-23. (This material is copyright 1990 by Liturgical Press and published by Liturgical Press, Collegeville, Minnesota. It is reprinted here with permission.)

An Alternative Prayer of Consecration Said at the Lord's Supper in the Sixth Century

The Liturgy of John Chrysostom was probably brought to Constantinople from Antioch by John Chrysostom himself when he became archbishop in 398.[1] It was then adapted to the liturgical style of Constantinople. In the sixth century, it was less frequently used than the Liturgy of Basil of Caesarea. But by the eleventh century, it was the principal liturgy, though the liturgy of Basil continued to be used for the most significant occasions, such as Easter and Christmas. While the anaphoras of both liturgies are prayers of thanksgiving that honor God by reciting salvation history, they do so by using different Bible verses. The anaphora of John Chrysostom focuses on God's loving gift of his Son for the world's salvation, quoting John 3:16. This anaphora is less developed than Basil's. It recounts the creation and the fall in only a cursory way. It expresses its Trinitarian theology not through theological formulation but through structure, devoting one section to the work of each Person of the Trinity. It thanks the Father for creation and redemption, remembers the saving work of the Son, and prays for the presence of the Holy Spirit in the liturgy and the church. Note: The present translation was made by R. C. D. Jasper and G. J. Cuming from the oldest Greek manuscript, Barb. Gr. 336 from the eighth century. Material from later manuscripts and printed editions not found in the earliest manuscript, including the people's parts, has been put in angle brackets (⟨ ⟩), while material from the early manuscript not found in later versions has been put in square brackets ([ ]).

"Priest" is an accurate translation of the word used in the eighth-century manuscript. In the context of sixth-century Constantinople, we should read "patriarch" or "bishop."

Priest:

The grace of our Lord Jesus Christ, and the love of God the Father, and the fellowship of the Holy Spirit be with you all.

People:

And with your spirit.

Priest:

Let us lift up our hearts.

People:

We have them with the Lord.

---

1. Robert F. Taft, "St. John Chrysostom and the Byzantine Anaphora That Bears His Name," in *Essays in Early Eastern Eucharistic Prayers,* ed. Paul F. Bradshaw (Collegeville, Minn.: The Liturgical Press, 1997), pp. 195-226, esp. 206-17.

Priest:

Let us give thanks to the Lord.

People:

It is fitting and right ⟨to worship the Father, the Son, and the Holy Spirit, the consubstantial and undivided Trinity⟩.

The priest begins the holy anaphora:

It is fitting and right to hymn you, ⟨to bless you, to praise you,⟩ to give you thanks, to worship you in all places of your dominion. For you are God, ineffable, inconceivable, invisible, incomprehensible, existing always and in the same way, you and your only-begotten Son and your Holy Spirit. You brought us out of nonexistence into existence; and when we had fallen, you raised us up again, and did not cease to do everything until you had brought us up to heaven, and granted us the kingdom that is to come. For all these things we give thanks to you and to your only-begotten Son and to your Holy Spirit, for all that we know and do not know, your seen and unseen benefits that have come upon us.

We give you thanks also for this ministry; vouchsafe to receive it from our hands, even though thousands of archangels and ten thousands of angels stand before you, cherubim and seraphim, with six wings and many eyes, flying on high, *(aloud)* singing the triumphal hymn ⟨proclaiming, crying, and saying⟩:

People:

Holy, ⟨holy, holy, Lord of Sabaoth; heaven and earth are full of your glory. Hosanna in the highest. Blessed is he who comes in the name of the Lord. Hosanna in the highest⟩.

The priest, privately:

With these powers, Master, lover of man, we also cry and say: holy are you and all-holy, and your only-begotten Son, and your Holy Spirit; holy are you and all-holy and magnificent is your glory; for you so loved the world that you gave your only-begotten Son, that all who believe in him may not perish, but have eternal life.

When he had come and fulfilled all the dispensation for us, on the night in which he handed himself over, he took bread in his holy and undefiled and blameless hands, gave thanks, blessed, broke, and gave it to his holy disciples and apostles, saying *(aloud)*, "Take, eat; this is my body, which is ⟨broken⟩ for you ⟨for forgiveness of sins⟩."

People:

Amen.

This prayer shares an essential quality with much ancient praying: commemoration of God's saving activity. These Eucharistic prayers present condensed summaries of the whole biblical story of salvation. Often this first part of a Eucharistic prayer is called the preface, not simply because it precedes the rest of the prayer, but because it proclaims (the Latin word *praefatio* can mean "proclamation") God's tremendous deeds.

The frequent use of instructions such as "aloud" and "privately" in the ninth-century text from which these prayers were translated shows that by then most of the Eucharistic prayer was said silently. In the sixth century there was a disagreement about whether this prayer should be said loud enough so that the people could hear it. (See p. 134.)

The priest, privately:

Likewise the cup also after supper, saying *(aloud),* "Drink from this, all of you; this is my blood of the new covenant, which is shed for you and for many for the forgiveness of sins."

People:

Amen.

The priest, privately:

We therefore, remembering this saving commandment and all the things that were done for us: the cross, the tomb, the resurrection on the third day, the ascension into heaven, the session at the right hand, the second and glorious coming again; *(aloud)* offering you your own from your own, in all and for all,

People:

we hymn you, ⟨we bless you, we give you thanks, Lord, and pray to you, our God⟩.

The priest says privately:

We offer you also this reasonable and bloodless service, and we pray and beseech and entreat you, send down your Holy Spirit on us and on these gifts set forth; and make this bread the precious body of your Christ, ⟨changing it by your Holy Spirit,⟩ Amen; and that which is in this cup the precious blood of your Christ, changing it by your Holy Spirit, Amen; so that they may become to those who partake for vigilance of soul, for fellowship with the Holy Spirit, for the fullness of the kingdom ⟨of heaven⟩, for boldness toward you, not for judgment or condemnation.

We offer you this reasonable service also for those who rest in faith, ⟨forefathers,⟩ fathers, patriarchs, prophets, apostles, preachers, evangelists, martyrs, confessors, ascetics, and all the righteous ⟨spirits⟩ perfected in faith; *(aloud)* especially our all-holy, immaculate, highly glorious, Blessed Lady, Mother of God, and ever-Virgin Mary; ⟨*diptychs of the dead;*⟩ Saint John the ⟨prophet,⟩ forerunner, and Baptist, and the holy, ⟨glorious,⟩ and honored Apostles; and this saint whose memorial we are keeping; and all your saints: at their entreaties, look on us, O God.

And remember all those who have fallen asleep in hope of resurrection to eternal life ⟨*he remembers them by name*⟩, and grant them rest where the light of your own countenance looks upon them.

Again we beseech you, remember, Lord, all the orthodox episcopate who rightly divide the word of your truth, all the priesthood, the diaconate in Christ, and every order of the clergy.

We offer you this reasonable service also for the (whole) world, for the holy, catholic, and

---

Some statement of offering to God in light of the commemoration of salvation history in Jesus Christ is a standard part of Eucharistic prayers, ancient and modern.

The double offering shows how this anaphora — brought to Constantinople from Antioch by John Chrysostom — was adapted to local custom. The offering of "your own from your own" with its response, which the people were used to singing, was added to a prayer whose own offering was of "reasonable and bloodless service." The opening dialogue, the people's responses, and the concluding doxology form the consistent frame shared by both these Eucharistic prayers.

apostolic church, for those who live in a chaste and reverent state, [for those in mountains and in dens and in caves of the earth,] for the most faithful Emperor, the Christ-loving Empress, and all their court and army: grant them, Lord, a peaceful reign, that in their peace we may live a quiet and peaceful life in all godliness and honesty.

Remember, Lord, the city in which we dwell, and all cities and lands, and all who dwell in them in faith.

(aloud) Above all, remember, Lord, our Archbishop *N.*

As in the anaphora of Basil, a deacon would read the diptychs of the dead and the living aloud while the presider continued the prayer in a low voice.

Diptychs of the living

Remember, Lord, those at sea, travelers, the sick, those in adversity, prisoners, and their salvation.

Remember, Lord, those who bring forth fruit and do good works in your holy churches, and remember the poor; and send out your mercies upon us all, *(aloud)* and grant us with one mouth and one heart to glorify and hymn your all-honorable and magnificent name, the Father, the Son, and the Holy Spirit, ⟨now and always and to the ages of ages.⟩

People:

Amen.

Source: The Liturgy of John Chrysostom is available in Greek in F. E. Brightman, *Liturgies: Eastern and Western* (Oxford: Clarendon Press, 1896; reprint ed., 1965), pp. 309-44. Brightman bases much of his text on the earliest surviving manuscript of these liturgies, Barberini Gr. 336 (8th century), which can be found in a critical edition titled *L'eucologio Barberini Gr. 336,* ed. Stefano Parenti and Elena Velkovska (Rome: C.L.V. — Edizioni Liturgiche, 1995). The English translation of the anaphora of Chrysostom reproduced here is from *Prayers of the Eucharist: Early and Reformed,* 3rd ed., ed. R. C. D. Jasper and G. J. Cuming (Collegeville, Minn.: The Liturgical Press, 1992), pp. 131-34. (This material is copyright 1990 by Liturgical Press and published by Liturgical Press, Collegeville, Minnesota. It is reprinted here with permission.)

SERMONS

A Sung Sermon Showing the Nature of Byzantine Piety around Christ's Birth

The following piece was composed by Romanos, a deacon in the Church of the Mother of God in a northern district of Constantinople. Romanos, who died in the third quarter of the sixth century, brought to the capital from his native Syria the tradition of liturgical poetry, in which even sermons were composed with meter and rhyme. The most famous of the Syriac verse sermons are those by Ephrem (4th c., Edessa). Romanos composed numerous kontakia, which were sermons in verse that were chanted to music. The precise manner of musical performance cannot be recovered. As with Byzantine psalmody, the short refrain at the end of each verse may have been a way for all the people to join in the singing. Although these pieces were not composed for Hagia Sophia, they do show the nature of early Byzantine piety and love for God. Full kontakia are no longer used in Byzantine worship, but some of the preludes and first stanzas are. The following kontakion on Christmas, consisting mainly of a dialogue between Mary and the magi, was the poet's best-known work and the one that brought him to public attention. The recurring refrain ("a little Child, God before the ages") illuminates the paradox of the Christmas proclamation: God is revealed as a little child come to save. The tale is told with intimacy and with strokes of cosmic breadth.

Prelude

Today the Virgin gives birth to him who is above all being,

and the earth offers a cave to him whom no one can approach.

Angels with shepherds give glory,

and magi journey with a star,

for to us there has been born

    a little Child, God before the ages.

1. Bethlehem has opened Eden, come, let us see;

    we have found delight in secret, come, let us receive

    the joys of Paradise within the cave.

    There the unwatered root whose blossom is forgiveness has appeared.

    There has been found the undug well

    from which David once longed to drink.

    There a virgin has borne a babe

This kontakion would have been sung at the night vigil that preceded the celebration of Christ's birth. Right away Romanos makes his hearers contemporaries with the action in the Gospel story.

The "unwatered root" in verse one is probably an allusion to Christ as the suffering servant of Isaiah, who "grew up . . . like a root out of dry ground" (Isa. 53:2). "Undug well" probably alludes to 2 Samuel 23:15, where David longs to drink from the "well of Bethlehem." Byzantine hymnography loves such paradoxical expressions.

and has quenched at once Adam's and David's thirst.

For this, let us hasten to this place where there has been born

a little Child, God before the ages.

2.   The mother's Father has willingly become her Son,

the infants' savior is laid as an infant in a manger.

As she who bore him contemplates him, she says,

"Tell me, my Child, how were you sown, or how were you planted in me?

I see you, my flesh and blood, and I am amazed,

because I give suck and yet I am not married.

And though I see you in swaddling clothes,

I know that the flower of my virginity is sealed,

for you preserved it when, in your good pleasure, you were born

a little Child, God before the ages.

3.   "High King, what have you to do with beggars?

Maker of heaven, why have you come to those born of earth?

Did you love a cave or take pleasure in a manger?

See, there is no place for your servant in the inn.

I do not say a place, not even a cave,

for that too belongs to another.

To Sara, when she bore a child,

a vast land was given as her lot. To me, not even a foxhole.

I used a cavern where willingly you made your dwelling,

a little Child, God before the ages."

4.   As she spoke such words in secret

and entreated the One who knows what is hidden,

she heard the magi seeking the babe.

At once, the Maiden cried to them, "Who are you?"

They answered her, "And you, who are you,

that you have borne such a Child?

Who is your father, who is she who bore you,

that you have become mother and nurse of a son without father?

On seeing his star we understood that there had appeared

a little Child, God before the ages.

The paradoxes here recall the central paradox of salvation as Byzantine thought understands it: God lived a human life so that humans may enjoy divine life. Wonder at the mystery of the Incarnation is often expressed through reflection on Mary's role in it.

Early Christians traditionally located the manger of Luke's Gospel in a cave.

Romanos focuses on the account of the Nativity from Matthew, not Luke, as Matthew's account was the main Gospel reading for Christmas in Constantinople.

5. "For Balaam laid before us precisely

   the meaning of the words he spoke in prophecy,

   when he said that a Star would dawn,

   a Star that quenches all prophecies and auguries;

   a Star that resolves the parables of the wise,

   and their sayings and their riddles,

   a Star far more brilliant than the star

   which has appeared, for he is the maker of all the stars,

   of whom it was written of old, 'From Jacob, there dawns

   > a little Child, God before the ages.'"

The contrast here is between the star of Bethlehem and the Star of Balaam's prophecy, which is Christ (cf. Num. 24:17).

6. When Mary heard these amazing words,

   she bowed low and worshiped the offspring of her womb

   and with tears, she said, "Great, my Child,

   great is all that you have done for me in my poverty;

   for see, magi are outside seeking you.

   The kings of the East seek your face,

   and the rich among your people beg to see you,

   for truly your people are those to whom you have been made known as

   > a little Child, God before the ages.

By this point of the sermon, it is obvious that Romanos is retelling the story of Christ's birth as a theological narrative that seeks to invite his listeners into the story and to identify with the characters. Note that his telling of the Christmas story is not mainly one of sentimentality but one of theological interpretation of the significance of the Incarnation.

7. "So, since they are your people, my Child, bid them

   come under your roof, that they may see

   rich poverty, precious beggary.

   You I have as glory and pride; therefore I am not ashamed.

   You are the grace and beauty

   of my dwelling and of me. Nod and let them enter.

   My poverty does not worry me;

   I hold you as a treasure that the kings have come to see,

   for kings and magi know that you have appeared

   > a little Child, God before the ages."

Romanos continues to play with the theme of the star, bringing it into the present. The power of the star, which is the Star who is Christ, continues to burn in the Gospel, drawing people to himself.

8. Jesus the Christ and truly our God

   secretly touched his mother's mind,

   saying, "Bring in those I have brought by my word,

   for it is my word which shone on those who were seeking me.

   To the senses it is a star, but to the mind a power.

   It accompanied the magi as my minister,

and still stands fulfilling its service

and showing with its rays the place where there has been born

    a little Child, God before the ages.

<table>
<tr>
<td>

More paradoxes reflect on the mystery of the Incarnation. Christ is a baby in his mother's arms yet remains the God who is everywhere (cf. John 10:7-9).

</td>
<td>

9. "Therefore now receive, holy Lad — receive those who have received me,

for I am in them as I am in your arms;

I did not leave you and yet I came with them."

She opens the door and receives the company of the magi.

She opens the door — she, the unopened

gate through which Christ alone has passed.

She opens the door — she who was opened

and yet in no way robbed of the treasure of her purity.

She opened the door, she from whom was born the door,

    a little Child, God before the ages.

</td>
</tr>
<tr>
<td>

This "unopened gate" is a reference to Ezekiel 44:2 from Ezekiel's vision of the new Temple, a verse often applied to Mary in Byzantine theology and liturgy. Here and elsewhere Romanos refers to the doctrine of the perpetual virginity of Mary. This belief is based on Scripture (e.g., Ezekiel 44:2) and theology. Through the Incarnation, Mary obtained full union with God, making the marital image of that union of no value for her as a means of salvation.

</td>
<td>

10. The magi at once hastened into the room

and, seeing Christ, they trembled as they saw

his mother and her betrothed.

And in fear they said, "This is a son without ancestry.

And how is it, O Virgin, that at this moment we see

your betrothed within your house?

Was your conceiving blameless?

Will people not find fault at Joseph's living with you?

You have a multitude of jealous people enquiring where there has been born

    a little Child, God before the ages."

</td>
</tr>
<tr>
<td>

The story of Christ's birth continues to be the one from Matthew's Gospel (see Matt. 1:18-24).

</td>
<td>

11. "I will tell you," Mary said to the magi,

"why I keep Joseph in my house:

to refute all those who slander me.

He will tell what he has heard about my Child.

For in his sleep he saw a holy angel

who told him how I had conceived.

In the night a fiery vision told

the creature of thorn about the things which grieved him.

That is why Joseph is with me, to show that there is

    a little Child, God before the ages.

</td>
</tr>
</table>

12. "He proclaims clearly all he has heard.

He declares openly all that he has seen in heaven and on earth:

the story of the shepherds, how beings of fire sang praises with ones of clay,

that of you, magi, how a star hastened before you,

lighting your way and guiding you.

And so, leaving aside all that you said before,

now recount to us what has befallen you.

Where have you come from; how did you understand that there had appeared

      a little Child, God before the ages?"

Apart from the manger, this is the sole reference in the body of the hymn to Luke's story of Christ's birth (see Luke 2:8-14). It reflects a favored theme of Byzantine liturgy — namely, that in worship humans join the heavenly liturgy.

13. When the Shining One had spoken thus,

the lamps of the East said to her,

"Do you wish to learn from where we have come here?

From the land of the Chaldeans, where they do not say, 'The Lord is God of gods.'

From Babylon, where they do not know

who is the maker of the things they reverence.

From there it came, the spark from your Child,

and raised us from the Persian fire;

we have left an all-devouring fire and see a fire which brings dew:

      a little Child, God before the ages.

Fire played a major role in Zoroastrianism, the religion of the Persian Empire. The reference to Persia would have been of special significance to the citizens of sixth-century Constantinople. At the time, Persia was the Roman Empire's main foe in the east, and the two empires were frequently at war (see Timeline, pp. 6-9).

14. "Everything is vanity of vanities.[1]

But there is none among us who thinks this,

for some deceive while others are deceived.

Therefore, Virgin, thanks be to your Offspring,

through whom we have been freed,

not only from deception but from hardship

in all the countries through which we passed,

of nations unknown, of tongues incomprehensible,

as we wandered through the earth and searched it,

with the lamp of the star seeking out where there had been born

      a little Child, God before the ages.

15. "But while we still had this lamp,

we journeyed through all Jerusalem,

fitly fulfilling the words of the prophecy.

For we had heard that God had threatened to search her thoroughly,

and with the lamp we wandered,

---

1. Compare Ecclesiastes 1:2.

wishing to find a great judgment.[2]

But it was not found, because her Ark

had been taken away with all the good things it had held before.

The things of old have passed away, for he has renewed all things,

    a little Child, God before the ages."

16. Mary, Scripture says, said to the faithful magi,

    "So, have you journeyed through all Jerusalem,

that city which slays prophets?

How did you pass unharmed through the city malevolent to all?

How did you avoid Herod,

who breathes out murder, not justice?"

But they answered her, "Virgin,

we did not avoid him, we mocked him.

We met them all and asked where there had been born

    a little Child, God before the ages."

17. When the Mother of God heard this from them,

    she said to them, "What did King Herod and the Pharisees ask you?"

"First Herod, then, as you said, the leaders of your nation

inquired of us exactly the time

of this star which is now visible.

And when they knew, as though they had not learned,

they had no desire to see the one of whom they sought to learn

because, for those who seek, there must be seen

    a little Child, God before the ages.

18. "They thought us mad, the fools,

    and asked, 'From where have you come and when?

And how have you journeyed by unseen paths?'

But we in turn asked them what they already knew,

'But how did you of old journey through

the great desert which you crossed?

He who guided those who came from Egypt

himself now guides those who come to him from Chaldea;

then by a pillar of fire, now by the star which shows

    a little Child, God before the ages.'"[3]

2. The allusion here appears to be to Zephaniah 1:12.
3. There is some question about the authenticity of verse 19 of this kontakion. For this reason it is not

20. These things were spoken by the unerring magi,

    and they were all sealed by the holy Virgin.

    And what both had said was confirmed by the infant;

    he left her womb unsullied after childbirth,

    and showed their mind, like their steps,

    unwearied after their coming.

    For none of them had undergone toil,

    as Avvakoum had not been wearied when he came to Daniel.

    For he who appeared to the prophets was the same who appeared to the magi,

        a little Child, God before the ages.

Avvakoum is the Greek form of the name of Habakkuk, the prophet. In the Septuagint version of the book of Daniel, God tells Habakkuk to bring food from Judea to Daniel in the lions' den in Babylon.

21. When they had told all their story,

    the magi took the gifts in their hands and worshiped

    the Gift of gifts, the Myrrh of myrrh.

    They brought Christ gold and myrrh and then incense

    and cried, "Accept our triple gift,

    as you do the Thrice Holy Hymn of the seraphim.

    Do not reject them like those of Cain,

    but embrace them like Abel's offering,

    through her who gave you birth, and through whom you have been born for us,

        a little Child, God before the ages."

Earthly worship is joined to heavenly worship. The "Thrice Holy Hymn" is the "Holy, Holy, Holy" of Isaiah's vision (Isa. 6:3). It is a hymn encountered frequently and in various forms in Byzantine worship. (See pp. 84, 94.)

22. When the blameless Virgin saw the magi bringing

    new and radiant gifts and worshiping,

    the star showing him, the shepherds praising him,

    she implored the Maker and Creator of all these, saying,

    "Accept, my Child, a trinity of gifts;

    grant her who gave you birth three requests.

    I pray to you for the seasons

    and for the fruits of the earth and for those who dwell in it.

    Be reconciled to all, because through me you have been born

        a little Child, God before the ages.

23. "For I am not simply your mother, compassionate Savior;

    it is not in vain that I suckle the giver of milk,

    but for the sake of all I implore you.

---

included in Lash's translation. The Schorck translation, however, does provide a version of verse 19.

Byzantine piety and theology recognize a special place for Mary within the worshiping church because of her unique relationship with Christ. She is his mother, to whom her son listens, as at the wedding in Cana (John 2:1-11). More than this, by the Incarnation she has become the first to obtain full union with God, the perfection of faith, so that her prayers will always be granted (cf. Matt. 21:21-22).

You have made me the mouth and the boast of all my race,

and your world has me as a mighty protection, a wall and a buttress.

They look to me, those who were cast out

of the Paradise of pleasure, for I bring them back.

May all things understand that, through me, you have been born

    a little Child, God before the ages.

24. "Save the world, O Savior. For this you have come.

Set your whole universe aright. For this, you have shone

on me and on the magi and on all creation.

For see, the magi, to whom you have shown the light of your face,

fall down before you and offer gifts,

useful, fair, and eagerly sought.

For I have need of them, since I am about

to go to Egypt and to flee with you and for you,

my guide, my Son, my Maker, my Redeemer,

    a little Child, God before the ages."

Source: Romanos's sermon on the Nativity is found in St. Romanos the Melodist, *Kontakia: On the Life of Christ,* trans. Archimandrite Ephrem Lash (San Francisco: HarperCollins, 1995), pp. 3-12. (Rights to this volume are held by the International Sacred Literature Trust, London, England.) Lash based his translation on the critical edition provided by Paul Maas and Constantine Trypanis in *Sancti Romani Melodi Cantica* (Oxford: Clarendon Press, 1963). Another critical edition is that by José Grosdidier de Matons published as Romanos le Mélode, *Hymnes,* 5 volumes, Sources chrétiennes (Paris: Les Éditions du Cerf, 1964-81). Other English translations of Romanos are found in R. J. Schork, *Sacred Song from the Byzantine Pulpit: Romanos the Melodist* (Gainesville: University Press of Florida, 1995). Only Schork has a translation of stanza 19, which may not be original to the Kontakion.

A Sung Sermon by Romanos Showing an Understanding of Baptism

The following kontakion by Romanos explores the meanings of baptism by portraying salvation in cosmic terms in relationship to large biblical narratives, especially that of the Garden of Eden. In this explanation, the kontakion reflects emphases found in the Byzantine baptismal rite, which, like many ancient rites, cast baptism as a renunciation of Satan and his realm and allegiance to Christ and the Kingdom of God, all put within a framework of biblical salvation history. In stanzas 4-10, the evil angel Belial (see 2 Cor. 6:15) decries the salvation he sees God working in baptism. The kontakion ends with exhortations for the newly baptized to be true to what they have received and experienced in the baptismal waters.

Prelude

Children of the baptismal font, all newly baptized,

as you are giving thanks, let us cry out to Thee, Christ, God,

"Baptize us in the light of Thy countenance,

clothe us in the robe worthy of Thy marriage.

Glory to Thee, glory to Thee, because Thou hast consented to

    Our resurrection."[1]

> Baptism is often compared with marriage in Eastern Christian thought. The goal of baptism is union with God in Christ. Sometimes the robe of baptism refers to the Holy Spirit.

1. Who can tell, who can show to Adam, the first-created,

    the beauty, the pride, the power of his children?

    Again, who can describe to suffering Eve

    that her descendants were made rulers,

    possessing the robe of glory, and that with much honor

    they extol the One in glory, as they shine forth in body,

    in spirit, and in stately bearing?

    Marvel of marvels, those who were formerly men

    suddenly are angels; men of clay now fiery beings.

    Indeed, who exalts them? It is entirely

        Our resurrection.

> By referencing Adam and Eve and speaking of the elevation of their descendants, Romanos places the significance of baptism into a larger frame of reference than just a single individual's experience. In Romanos's estimation, a cosmic story of salvation history is the context for understanding what is truly happening in the church's sacraments.

2. No longer are they thrust out as strangers of the holy ones,[2]

    but now all who heard "Come unto me"[3] are His own.

    No longer do they stand outside the bridal chamber,

1. The refrain "Our resurrection" is a name both for baptism and for Christ (cf. John 11:25).
2. This is probably an allusion to Ephesians 2:19 but also to Adam and Eve's expulsion from Eden (Genesis 3:23-24).
3. See Matthew 11:28.

because they have entered in[to] that bridal chamber;

no longer are they frustrated, but they are of good cheer;

no longer as spies, but truly as bishops

as they are claimed by the holy ones.

No longer do they knock at the door, crying:

"O Merciful One, open the door," but they worship from within:

"Thou who hast shed light on us all,

     Our resurrection."

In verse 3, Romanos is alluding to the Eastern notion of *theosis* or divinization. It is an understanding of salvation that emphasizes human participation in the divine nature (cf. 2 Pet. 1:4), which comes about through union with God. It is premised on a certain understanding of the significance of Christ's Incarnation: He has taken on human nature so that humans might participate in divine nature.

3.   Nature, which had been abased, was exalted;

it was exalted, magnified, and achieved divine creation.

Man became god, possessing God;

he found the One whom he sought in Paradise.

Since he asked for something else, he was changed into something else.

Since he sought it, indeed he became royal and bore the title of God.

There he thirsted and there he drank.

There was his longed-for goal, and he reached it;

and who gave these things to him? Surely

     Our resurrection.

4.   Adam, you are clear, you are radiant and worthy of emulation;

when he hated you, you slipped from his malignant eye,

for on seeing you, the tyrant [Belial] weakened and cried out:

"Who is this whom I see? I do not understand.

The heap of earth is renewed, dust has been deified,

the poor and the least among you has been called and washed,

and even the one who lost heart as he entered.

He is drawn to the table, he dared to eat,

and he did not fear to drink the One who Himself created him.

Indeed, who has shown this to him? Surely

     Your resurrection.

These lines prepare for the list of Old Testament water events in the next stanzas. The salvific character of baptism was not revealed until Christ's resurrection (see John 5:1-9).

5.   "He does not remember a man's old sins;

he did not allow the pain of former wounds to appear at all.

Just as the paralytic long ago cast aside

his paralysis, leaving it at the side of the baptismal font,

he no longer carried his bed on his shoulders,

but he brings with him the cross of the One who showed mercy

to me and died.

Many times before this, as a lover of men, did He

baptize many men in waters, and so they were not conspicuous.

Now they have been revealed as radiant by

> Your resurrection.

6. "The streams of water of the ever-flowing Source in Paradise

in truth divide into rivers,

and in them the sickened Adam, as is written,

did not assuage one pain.

At the time of Noah, the flood deluged the earth,

but it did not wipe clean the one formerly sickened,

but rather drowned him.

Indeed, what happened that the waters

ignored going to the depths and learned how to save?

Truly this is what transformed it: namely,

> Your resurrection.

Romanos uses an ancient method of biblical interpretation called **typology**, finding parallels (or, in this case, contrasts) between baptismal waters and stories of water in the Bible. The point here, one of the evil angel's complaints, is to wonder how baptismal waters gained the power to save since biblical waters seemed to destroy. The answer is that everything has been transformed by the Resurrection. To relate baptism and watery episodes from the Bible, usually in a positive correspondence, was a common feature of ancient preaching.

7. "Lo, I see more of the Red Sea;

it was revealed to the depths of the sea, passable for all men,

but it did not baptize them, nor save them from sin;

yet it did baptize, and it did save them.

However, in this case, it did not save all men, only the people

whom the waters revealed, but it is now exposed for each person

and for all races.

They were not turned back; they were not separated from one another.

You are not an Egyptian, are you? Whoever you are, come,

For living water has shown

> Your resurrection.

The difference between the waters of the Exodus and baptism is that baptism saves all, even the Egyptians.

8. "The source of a very evil stream was once cured

by Elisha, the very wise prophet.

He treated the waters; their taste

had the plague of barrenness.[4]

But even though the waters were cured and changed,

4. See 2 Kings 2:19-22.

they did not know how to purify sins

and renew the spirit.

However, baptismal waters learned this: they both purified all men

and they were for all who were born a bath of rebirth,

and this bestowed the gift of life,

       Your resurrection.

A common theme in Byzantine hymnography is that Christ's resurrection has despoiled hell, liberating those held captive by death and the devil. Belial laments that all his captives — the poor, the rich, the deformed, slaves, despots (or masters), transgressors — are being taken from him. Even he was given the opportunity to repent, he says in verse 10.

9.   "I do not know what to say, I do not know what to do;

difficulties are everywhere for me; I am in doubt as to what I see;

grace without a giving; a gift without a gift;

who is not overwhelmed at this?

Is the poor man able to hesitate or the rich man to flag in weariness?

Are the deformed ashamed? Are slaves not urged forward?

Do despots not hasten?

All men come, for they heard

the Master saying: 'The well of water I give is eternal.

I baptize all and cleanse them, I,

       Your resurrection.'

10.   "Let us rouse up all who have fallen asleep in deepest Hades.

The sound of this lamentation is like a mountain torrent;

He raised up those from among the transgressors,

and He even approached me.

He cleansed the filthy and those without money;

He made all men wealthy, and He took from them only a word

in return for what He gave them.

'I believe,' they said; and they received everything.

They breathed upon me, and thus they cried out:

'We believe that it saves us,

       Our resurrection.'"

In the Byzantine baptismal liturgy, those about to be baptized are told to renounce and breathe (or, in later times, breathe and spit) on Satan, a gesture of repudiation. They do this while facing toward the west. They then turn toward the east, attach themselves to Christ, and recite the Creed: "I believe...." In this way, the baptismal candidates physically enact their conversion.

Neophytes are newly baptized Christians.

11.   As Belial saw the group receiving these words —

those who were a while ago **neophytes** —

now even more than formerly he shrewdly pays attention

To the child of the baptismal font.

And so, now I call upon you, since I love you more,

O Neophyte, dear to me, always be what you have been called,

one newly baptized everywhere,

pleasing on every occasion, beautiful always,

not a bridegroom today and unwed tomorrow,

for this has married you to the Lord,

>> Our resurrection.

Note the recurring use of marriage imagery as a way of understanding baptism.

12. As you say, "I believe," continue believing;

and as I command, so govern yourself outside.

Do not take off your glory with your robe;

remain white-robed in your spirit.

Do not let the deceiver say to you, "Only for seven days

do you need to stay with the One who first gave you orders;

after that go away."

But just as you learned, and as you sang with rejoicing,

"If you heard His voice today,"

Just so, sing a hymn each day to

>> Our resurrection.

Romanos exhorts the newly baptized to remain faithful to what it is they have received and to what they have become in baptism. The specific liturgical references are to practices of clothing new Christians in white robes and maintaining the week after baptism as a special time of worship.

13. For you did not come because necessity was imposed on you,

nor did you come because someone else forcibly dragged you in,

but you attached yourself to Him when you heard Him say,

"Come unto me, ye who thirst, and drink."[5]

And only as you came were you asked this:

"Do you believe, O man, that I possess the spring of life?"[6]

You answered, "I believe."

The saints were present, and the angels were there too.

The powers stood by, powers and thrones heard

you crying that "I believe

>> Our resurrection."

At times in this text the Greek term translated "man" or "men" is better translated "human being(s)." There is no intentional reference to a particular sex.

14. But if you can deny this before them,

guard yourself, friend, and fortify yourself in every way.

Do not acquire for yourself accusers above and below,

for all creation heard you.

But many times in fear of those who control the laws,

you came to the baptismal font, and you became what you became,

ashamed of the occasion.

5. Compare John 7:37-38.
6. See John 4:10-15.

And what will happen to you when the occasion

of the Last Judgment will arrive, and everything will be brought to trial,

And you will explain in turn

Our resurrection?

15. Remind yourself, friend, of these things:

You approached in fear, remain in fear.

Love what you received, and keep what you possess.

Do not backslide to earlier behavior.

Do not become the laughingstock of the one who now dreads you,

for if you behold yourself acting as formerly,

rejoicing over you, the Devil will say,

"I do not attach you to me and to my service;

you did not love Christ, and you were clinging close to me;

you did not deny me as you said, 'I hold in reverence

Our resurrection.'"

Romanos envisions the time after baptism as one of a spiritual battle in which the devil tries to tempt the Christian by questioning the authenticity of the pledges made in baptism.

16. Therefore, in order that the enemy may not shame you,

and the Merciful One consider you as transgressor,

look to your armor, with which I shall now gird you;

consider things worthy of your beauty;

call to mind time after time who you are and what you became;

bear in mind on every occasion your first shabbiness

and your present kingdom;

do not forget, man, your descendants;

do not be judged foolish and like unto cattle;

mind everything and cry out with joy

Our resurrection.

In these verses, the poet assumes the role of the baptizing minister. The reference may be to the anointing for the gift of the Holy Spirit that immediately followed baptism.

17. The Creator considers you as son and heir;

for those whom the womb of the baptismal font has produced

the loving Father receives, He who is over all men,

and He has them registered as His heirs.

Then, lo, my brother, you have a certain Father;

cling to Him; do not leave the One who gave you birth

and who for the rest of time will be in charge of you,

crying, "Hear, I have engendered a son,

and having produced him, I shall exalt him though he transgressed, if he time after time cried to me: 'I hold in reverence

    Our resurrection.'"

18. Stretch every nerve toward the divine,

    For in truth you have been thought entirely worthy of sacred things.

    No share of glory is denied you,

    for all things have been consecrated for all.

    Do not corrupt your eyes with spectacles;

    do not let the mournful sound of the one who calls to destruction

    contaminate your ears;

    Do not defile your mouth with songs

    with which the enemy finds pleasure and with which the

    spirit is burdened;

    But on every occasion simply cry out and hymn

        Our resurrection.

> The recurring refrain of "Our resurrection" serves in the sermon not only as a simple interpretation of baptism's meaning (in baptism we have passed from death to life) but also as a title for Christ (see John 11:25) and a rallying cry to stay properly focused as the Christian aims for the consummation of God's Kingdom.

19. Lo, you have been renewed; you have been restored;

    never will you bend your back in sins.

    O Neophyte, you procured the cross as staff;

    with it make fast your youthful spirit.

    Bring it forward in your prayer, at your table,

    by your couch, bring it forward on all occasions,

    Neophyte, as your subject of boasting.

    For the demons, like wild dogs,

    howl on all sides. Cry out to them,

    "Holding my cross, I take a stand, loving

        Our resurrection."

> Romanos encourages frequently making the sign of the cross on oneself, which is a type of prayer.

20. Now, in order that you may herd together with Christ's flock,

    stay away from the wolves; do not mingle with the impure;

    you are a lamb of tender flesh; do not be hardened;

    do not slip from the rocks;

    do not let the wily one say to you, "Do not blame those whom you

    do not respect,"

    nor let him completely trip you up about occasions to

    be carefully observed and days to be watched.

    Be the master of all things . . . both what is not to be touched,

    and what to abstain from,

> Romanos continues to exhort the newly baptized to stay faithful.

for our servant has given you all things,

> Our resurrection.

21. He does not say once for all, "Withdraw from your God,"

but he deprives you of all divine aids bit by bit.

He shows you dreams, and through them he disturbs you,

and in your dreams he shows you yourself:

"Withdraw from this place; flee this tree;

honor this spring, for I follow it,

and I am going to be an angel."

Do not persuade yourself of these things; rescue yourself,

and consider, man, the demon angel.

Rather, trample him underfoot and hold in reverence

> Our resurrection.

The specific danger to the newly baptized that Romanos has in mind is to fall back into pagan beliefs and practices. Two centuries after the conversion of the emperor Constantine, pagan religion continued to influence society, and the Church continued to battle against it.

22. Be discreet; take heed hereafter of the affairs of the Lord,

for you were called by His name, and you are a trusted steward.

Summon the aid of the One who had faith in you

on behalf of the peace of our spirits.

Say to your Bridegroom who is now united with you,

"I fall before Thee. Nod consent and, as merciful, grant

peace to Thy world.

Grant Thy aid to Thy churches,

kindness to Thy shepherds, unity to the flocks,

in order that all men everywhere may hymn

> Our resurrection."

Romanos's last instructions echo a petition from the litany of the faithful of the Eucharistic liturgy: "For the peace of the whole world, for the welfare of the holy churches of God, and for the union of all, let us pray to the Lord." The goal of both the prayer and living out the baptismal commitment is the spread of God's praise.

Source: This translation of Romanos's sermon on baptism is found in Marjorie Carpenter, *Kontakia of Romanos, Byzantine Melodist,* II: *On Christian Life* (Columbia: University of Missouri Press, 1973), pp. 229-36. (This translation is reproduced here by permission of the University of Missouri Press, copyright 1970 by the Curators of the University of Missouri.) It is based on the edition by Paul Maas and Constantine Trypanis in *Sancti Romani Melodi Cantica* (Oxford: Clarendon Press, 1963).

A Pentecost Sermon Preached in Another of Constantinople's Churches

*The following sermon was preached by a presbyter named Leontius in the sixth century on the occasion of the feast of **Pentecost**, which celebrated the descent of the Holy Spirit. As is characteristic of Byzantine piety, the feast reveals a salvation that is grand in scope. Much of Leontius's reflection on God is caught up in images of water and fire. The preacher is eager, too, to speak about the Trinity on this feast which commemorates the coming of the Holy Spirit. In the absence of liturgical books from the period, we rely on sermons like this one to tell us how feasts were celebrated and what Bible readings were used.*

1. As many of you who make haste concerning the eternal grace of the present celebration, let us run forward to the spring of good, to Christ. It is the spring of which the prophet cried to the Father of light, "With you is the spring of life; in your light we shall see light" [Ps. 36:9]. That is, in your only-begotten Son we see the Holy Spirit.

   > This psalm verse forms a line in an ancient hymn known by its first words, "Glory to God in the Highest," which was sung in the popular service of Matins and therefore was very familiar to Leontius's audience. Leontius begins here, with Christ as spring, to prepare for his commentary on the "living water" of the day's Gospel reading from John 7.

2. The prophet did well, then, to call Christ the Master "spring." It is possible, friends, it is possible in different places to see a worldly spring which is silver-colored, and, if one bends over it, thanks to the purity of the water, to observe from above the pebbles in the deep lying on the bottom. When, on a summer day, this sun with its fiery golden bow rests its rays, spreading them over the back of the water without getting them wet, the traveler, on approaching such a spring, cannot pass it by immediately with impunity. Cupping his hands in place of a mixing bowl, and eagerly bending his whole body,

   he draws water,

   he cures his thirst,

   he soothes the burning heat,

   he moistens his overheated face,

   he collects his weakened senses,

   he gives room to his cramped spirit,

   he softens his stony heart,

   he forces his legs to walk again although they are unwilling to move.

3. This silver-colored spring

   often cures thirst,

   > but harms the spleen,

   and it often soothes burning heat,

   > but makes the liver ill,

   and it often restrains the soul when it wishes to leap out of the body,

   > but it stores up a chill in the chest and causes pain which lasts many years.

   > Leontius, having drawn from his listeners' experience of both the delights and the hazards of natural water, makes a contrast to Christ as the source of a better, living water.

Jesus Christ our Master, on the other hand — he who is rightly called "spring," not because he teems with silver-colored streams but because he forms lessons of God's rule into a lake — does not cure one part of the faithful and hurt the other part. Out of perfection he bestows the gift of perfection, granting these gifts to those who run towards him, which he himself possesses by borrowing from no one. Christ the Master does not send the faithful far off to draw the living water, but compels them to get it in the stomach of knowledge. You have just heard him saying: "If anyone thirst, let him come to me and drink. He who believes in me, as the Scripture has said, 'Out of his stomach shall flow rivers of living water'" [John 7:37-38].

4.   There is also, friend, a mother-spring of four flowing rivers in the paradise of Eden, but it has been hollowed out of the earth and has its stream from below, and dries up at the same time as the present life. Because there are no candidates for baptism present, the use of the water is superfluous. Jesus Christ our Master, on the other hand, the eternal spring,

is not sent up from earth,

but sent out from heaven;

he is not partly enclosed,

but is glorified everywhere;

he does not perish with the perishable,

but gives to those who perish the gift of imperishability.

Leontius uses typology, the comparison of things from the Old Testament with things from the New. The Old Testament type foreshadows and is surpassed by its New Testament fulfillment. Here the spring in Eden is a type of Christ, the Spring of life, the four rivers of paradise are types of the Four Gospels, and Eden is a type of the church.

5.   Only four rivers suckle the spring in the paradise of Eden: Geon, Phison, Tigris, Euphrates. These, however, are local and carry little water, and do not irrigate the entire earth, and in winter they flood, while in summer they carry little water, but the apostolic rivers belonging to the spring of the paradise of the church are great and boundless, even if Judas did grow cold. Consider with all of them too the four great rivers of the evangelists, Matthew, Luke, Mark, [and] John, who irrigate every village and native land and city with lessons of God. If "star differs from star in glory" [1 Cor. 15:41], according to the teaching of Paul, how do spiritual things not excel bodily things?

6.   What kind of thing is it that the paradise in Eden is found to have, which this meadow of the church carries and is recognized by?

There Adam hid himself like a runaway slave;

here Christ the Master is worshiped as God.

There Eve was struck with the heel;

here Mary is glorified.

There wood impregnated death;

here wood makes life flourish.

There a snake mouthed falsehood;

here the Holy Spirit instructs about God.

There law-giving was disobeyed;

here knowledge of God is strengthened.

There there was a garden of roses;

here there is virginity.

There there was a lily with white petals;

here there is the sheen of the soul of the newly illuminated.

There there were tree-climbing vines with large berries;

here there are men who love words.

There there was wild foliage;

here there are holy women.

There there was a spring without a voice;

here there are mighty-voiced rivers.

7. You have just heard the river Euphrates, I mean John the evangelist, shouting the words: "On the last day of the celebration, the great day, Jesus stood up and proclaimed the words, 'If anyone thirst, let him come to me and drink'" [John 7:37]. What do you say, friend? Rather, why do you delay? Christ is calling; let no one hesitate. The spring is shouting; let no one excuse himself. Let us all thirst, let us all approach, however much we draw, as much remains. Let us shout, friends of David, the words of David to the eternal spring as we say: "As the hart longs for springs of water, so my soul longs for you, O God" [Ps. 42:1].

8. The evangelist did well, then, to say: "On the last day of the celebration, the great day" [John 7:37]. He did well to call this celebration both "last" and "great," because it is last and great and first. It is the last for the Jews. The last things that happened to them were bad because of their outrage against Christ, and the shame of their face was unmasked. This is why, in rebuking their capital city, Jerusalem, the Lord said: "You had a harlot's face; you behaved shamelessly in front of all" [Jer. 3:3]. It is the last, then, for the Jews, the first for the Christians. Theirs are the lees, ours is the pure drink; theirs are the grapestones, ours are the vats.

9. The evangelist did well, then, to call this celebration "last" and "great." What is more splendid than this present celebration? Every celebration of the Master makes only the living rejoice; but this celebration of Pentecost makes not only the living rejoice, but it speaks to the dead as well.

To broaden the notion of the superiority of what is experienced in Christ, Leontius employs a series of anti-types to speak of the saving power of Christ, which can be experienced in the church.

The Byzantine reading for Pentecost was chosen from John 7 for two reasons: one, because Christ speaks about the gift of the Spirit, and two, because of the expression "the last day of the celebration, the great day." In the early Christian period, the day of Pentecost was the last day of a fifty-day period, beginning with Easter, that celebrated Christ's resurrection. By Leontius's day, the introduction of a feast of Ascension on the fortieth day after Easter had altered this practice.

Leontius is referring here to the practice of visiting the graves of departed Christians on the day of Pentecost. (See the note by paragraph 24 for more.)

This celebration of the Pentecost both illuminates the churches

and strews roses on the graves.

This celebration of Pentecost both perfumes the houses

and anoints the tombs.

What is more splendid than this celebration, on which the Holy Spirit, in making itself

manifest, gave as a gift to the apostles the illumination of tongues?

Today Christianity has taken root.

Today Judaism has dried up.

Today paganism is smoking.

Today heresy has been blocked.

Today divine dogma has been spread.

10. But some will quite possibly say: "And how is it that today heresy has been blocked, while divine dogma has been spread?"

At this point Leontius shifts the emphasis in his preaching to a defense of the doctrine of the Trinity. The specific heresy that he wishes to contradict is a questioning of the essential unity of the Three Persons. Pentecost is the occasion for this defense of the Trinity because at Pentecost the Third Person of the Trinity, the Holy Spirit, is manifested.

How? By means of the teaching of the Lord. Today the Lord has taught us more clearly by a palpable example that the Father and the Son and the Holy Spirit have one nature in three different hypostases. If no one is able to separate spring and water and river, how do the children of the heretics dare to divide the Father from the Son and the Son from the Holy Spirit? Are earthly things indivisible and the spiritual things divisible?

11. But some will quite possibly say: "And who is the spring? Who is the water? Who is the river?"

Who is the spring? The "Father of light" [James 1:17].

Who is the water? The only-begotten Son.

Who is the river? The Holy Spirit.

And from where is this evident? Take the proof not from my words, but from the holy Scriptures. And that the Father is a spring, listen to the Father himself crying out through the prophet in these words to the Jews, who have blasphemous and filthy pits: "They have forsaken me, the spring of living water, and hewn out pits for themselves, broken pits that cannot hold water" [Jer. 2:13]. That the Son is water, listen to him saying to the Samaritan woman: "Woman, if you knew the gift of God and who it is that is saying to you, 'Give me a drink,' you would have asked him and he would have given you living water" [John 4:10]. That the Holy Spirit is a river, you have just heard the Lord saying about him: "If anyone thirst, let him come to me, and drink. He who believes in me, as the Scripture has said, 'Out of his stomach shall flow rivers of living water'" [John 7:37-38]. Then the evangelist added the following, lest they think that the Lord was speaking of a river in the perceptible world: "This he said about the Spirit, which those who believed in him were about to receive" [John 7:39].

Have you seen an eternal spring of orthodoxy?

Have you seen the untroubled water of piety?

Have you seen an unmuddied river of the knowledge of God?

12. The evangelist did well, then, to call the present celebration of Pentecost "great," because it is great.

Today the apostles have steadfastness;

today the fishermen are sophists;

today the ignorant are teachers;

today the ones who have one language have several languages;

today the inarticulate speak good Greek;

today the gloomy are resplendent;

today the ones of clay are fiery;

today the anglers are theologians;

today the ones who drag the lake cast nets over the world;

today the ones who search after fish instruct people;

today the ones who flee beasts trample on demons;

today the ones without capital have much capital;

today the inactive are active;

today the poor are money lenders;

today the pursued are appealed to;

today the naked live royally;

today the ones hidden in a corner are discoursers in the assembly.

The reader should remember that preaching in this period was a give-and-take affair between the preacher and the congregation. One could imagine the interest level of worshipers increasing as Leontius developed this list of Pentecost-caused reversals. Could they have tried to anticipate where each line led by calling back to Leontius?

13. And why do I still go on at length? Today the ones who grieve at being orphans call out the name of their father. Listen attentively. When Christ the Master ascended into heaven under the gaze of the apostles and promised the river of the Holy Spirit to the apostles — it was fitting for the spring when it ascended to promise a river — the apostles rejoiced and made their souls like reservoirs. But they did not know the moment when the fire-bearing river would come; at his ascension the Lord indicated the promise of the Holy Spirit, but the moment that it would come he did not make known at all. Why? Because God does not work at fixed moments, but makes manifest when he wishes.

14. After the Lord's ascension, then, the apostles continued to have hope of the Holy Spirit and to unite themselves and achieve openness with each other. When they saw during the first and the second and the third day that the gift of the promise had not led to fulfillment, the apostles, moved by human considerations, began to say, as they discussed among themselves: "What are we to do, men and brothers? We have already

come to the end of this tenth day, and we see nothing of what the teacher said coming to fulfillment.

"How strange and improbable this is! Should we take up our former fishing, or should we wait a little longer for the promise? We are spending this tenth day doing nothing. How strange! How improbable! Elisha, the pupil of Elijah, the pupil of the pupil, began to work miracles immediately after having received the sheepskin, and we're doing nothing?

"How improbable! Surely Elijah wasn't more powerful than our teacher? Let us not dare to say this. On the mountain of the transfiguration we saw with our own eyes how not only Elijah but also Moses worshiped our teacher as God. How strange! How improbable! Elisha, who drove a yoke of oxen, began to work miracles immediately after having received a sharp-haired skin which had belonged to a dumb animal — what was fitting for one who was a worker of the law but that he inherit the sheepskin? — and we who are not pupils of a pupil but apostles of God are coming to the end of the tenth day and doing nothing?"

15. While the apostles were discussing these things among themselves and expecting that the promise of hope was still a long way off, look, all at once the doors of heaven opened, the armies of the powers of the archangels shouted, the sea of the air was confused by cowardice, the cymbals of the clouds sent forth a sound of royal shouts, every spot on earth was shaken by the earthquake like a reed by wind, [and] the unfathomable vault of the ocean was covered with a fiery cloth. And Luke, the author of the Acts of the Apostles, bears witness to my story when he says, as you have just heard: "When the day of Pentecost had come, the apostles were all together in one place. And suddenly a sound came from heaven like the rush of a mighty wind, and it filled all the house where they were sitting. And there appeared to them tongues as of fire, distributed and resting on each of them, and they began to speak in other tongues as the Spirit gave them utterance" [Acts 2:1-4]. *As* it *gave,* not as it was commanded.

16. Have you seen the greatness of the celebration?
Have you seen the gift of the Holy Spirit?
Have you seen the shame of the heretics who fight against the Spirit?
They celebrate Pentecost and shoot at the Spirit.
Who forges tongues, unless it be the one who forms tongues from clay?
Who makes a mouth great with a lathe, unless it be the one who made the ass articulate words?[1]

---

1. See Numbers 22:28.

Sidenotes:

Leontius has placed his listeners into the biblical story as the disciples who had seen Christ's ascension and had heard the promise of the coming Spirit. The "tenth day" refers to the fact that Pentecost occurs ten days after the Ascension.

Leontius begins to comment on the Epistle reading of the day, the story of Pentecost from the book of Acts.

Who instructs the ignorant unless it be the Holy Spirit alone?

But those on the other side will say immediately: "And from where is this evident, that the Holy Spirit gives wisdom and knowledge of tongues?"

From where? Listen to the Lord, heretic, speaking to his disciples many years ago: "Don't be anxious how you are to speak or what you are to say when they bring you before rulers and authorities, for it is not you who speak but the Spirit of my Father speaking in you" [Matt. 10:18-20].

17. What marvelous actions! It was in fire that the Holy Spirit descended, as fire it rested on each one of the apostles, and although it was fire, it did not burn the apostles, but enlightened them. Why? Because it was not a burning but an enlightening fire, or rather it was both burning and enlightening, burning the blasphemers, enlightening the pious. Just as worldly and material fire

> burns thorns,
>
> melts wax,
>
> dissolves lead,
>
> dries clay,
>
> makes silver shine,
>
> purifies gold,
>
> lights up a house,

so too does immaterial fire, the Holy Spirit,

> obliterate sins,
>
> make a greedy heart wither,
>
> obliterate a wily person,
>
> purify a soul which is repentant,
>
> make a believing man resplendent,
>
> light up the house of the church.

Having begun the sermon with a comparison of the saving superiority of Christ over "worldly" water, Leontius accomplishes a similar comparison between the Holy Spirit and regular fire. He is picking up on the description in the book of Acts of the flames of fire that appeared on the disciples.

18. To explain it differently: it was in fire that the Holy Spirit descended, so that we might know clearly that the Holy Spirit is of divine essence. The Lord himself, our God, is fire, according to the saying: "Our God is a consuming fire" [Heb. 12:29; Deut. 4:24; 9:3]. And wherever you look for God showing a divine sign and offering a mystery, you will find him doing this in fire. Thus it was when, leading the sons of Israel out of the land of Egypt, he put a pillar of fire beside them, a fire which did not destroy but acted as a guide. Thus it was, too, when making his first manifestation to Moses through the flame of the burning bush, God sent forth his own voice, not in order to hear but in order to teach. Thus it was, too, when manifesting himself to Daniel, God showed himself seated on a throne of fire, not in order to punish the prophet, but in order to show everywhere in what things God is.

While to modern ears Leontius's proof texts might sound strained, he is following early Christian practices of reading across Scripture with imaginative association. It was the same interpretive principle that allowed associating baptism with biblical stories of water, as we saw earlier. (See pp. 113, 115.)

19. But some will quite possibly say that those are the proofs of the Old Testament. "Show us," they say, "that in the New Testament, too, God works miracles in fire. These are indications from the Old Testament."

Listen, friend. If you don't know, learn; if you do know, remember. Quite possibly you remember, friend, that when God guided the Magi before all people he guided them by means of a star. It is clear to everyone that the star was fire. Similarly, the Lord called his own body, the body of the sacred table, a "burning coal." And when did he do this? Listen to Isaiah crying out many years ago: "One of the seraphim flew to me, having in his hand a coal which he had taken with tongs from the altar. And he touched my lips and said to me: 'See, this has touched your lips and will take away your transgressions and purge away your sins entirely'" [Isa. 6:6-7]. What kind of coal takes away sin, unless it be the communion of the Lord? In this way the Lord called the baptism of our resurrection "fire." And from where is this clear? Listen to John the Baptist crying out: "He who is coming after me is mightier than I; his sandals I am not worthy to carry. He will baptize you with the Holy Spirit and with fire" [Matt. 3:11]. This sums up everything best, that it was in fire that the Holy Spirit descended.

20. This marvelous working of the Holy Spirit the more intelligent among the Jews understood, and because the apostles, who before this spoke one language, offered in their native language without an interpreter the teachings of piety to each single one who approached them from differing countries, as you have just heard, the more intelligent among the Jews in their amazement began to say to each other: "Look, aren't all these who are speaking Galileans? How is it that we hear, each of us in our own dialect which we were born into? Parthians and Medes and Elamites and residents of Mesopotamia, Judea and Cappadocia, Pontus and Asia, Phrygia and Pamphylia, Egypt and the parts of Libya belonging to Cyrene, and visitors from Rome, both Jews and proselytes, Cretans and Arabians, we hear them recounting in our own tongues the mighty works of God" [Acts 2:7-11].

21. The Jews were amazed at the sight of the apostles speaking in many tongues. This is why in their amazement they said to each other: "Look, aren't all these who are speaking Galileans [Acts 2:7], poor and common men? Aren't they ignorant men and weavers of nets? Haven't we frequently bought fish from these men?

"Where do they get this knowledge from? Surely they haven't caught tongues in their nets instead of fish? But we saw them before this, speaking one language. From where do they utter the various languages of the world's store as from the purse of their throats? Where do they get this knowledge from? Now we know that their teacher is truly God. Now we know that the old has passed away; see, all the new has come [2 Cor. 5:17]. Peter is speaking good Greek, which Moses wasn't able to do. Haven't we heard him saying: 'I am feeble of speech and sluggish of tongue'? [Exod. 4:10]. And he requested exemption from the divine order to be a messenger, on the grounds of the thinness of his voice, and he did not receive improvement but remained with what nature had given him. Let us leave Moses behind and bless these men — rather let us glorify the God who is working wonders in them, him who, in order to benefit all in common, remodeled the fishermen's simple organ of speech according to the need of the one who approached them. What was provided for Abraham like this? These men have surpassed everyone.

They spit on money,

they despise fame,

they heal without being paid,

they fast continually,

they are resplendent like those who fare sumptuously,

they issue commands to the dead,

they banish illnesses, and they make demons disappear,

when forced into service they rejoice,

when slapped in the face they turn the other cheek as well;

they travel without a staff and a pouch and a double cloak;

gold and silver and bronze they do not even wish to hear about.

Let us run to these men who recount "the mighty works of God" [Acts 2:11]; let us turn away the rest, those who talk nonsense and are of no use."

22. This, then, is what the more intelligent among the Jews said, but the lawless Jews, on the other hand, who were moved by envy, for their part began to object, as you have just heard: "They are filled with sweet wine" [Acts 2:13]. What is the meaning of "they are filled with sweet wine"? It corresponds to "they are terribly drunk and therefore they make strange utterances." On hearing this, blessed Peter could no longer bear it, in that the torch of the Holy Spirit was finally moving within him. Standing up in their midst, as you have just heard, he began to speak: "Men of Judea and all who reside in Jerusalem, let this be known to you and give ear to my words. For these men are not drunk, as you suppose, for it is the third hour of the day" [Acts 2:14-15].

23. Blessed Peter did well to call the third hour as witness to his sobriety. And who is the third hour? The Holy Spirit. The first hour is the Father, because he awarded the law. The second hour is the Son, because he gave grace as a gift. The third hour is the Holy Spirit, because it made the apostles' tongues speak many languages.

Peter said, then: "Men of Judea and all who reside in Jerusalem, let this be known to you and give ear to my words. For these men are not drunk, as you suppose" [Acts 2:14-15] Nobody will think that the gift of God is drunkenness. Either smell or listen.

Leontius takes a step at this point beyond typology to allegory. Again, such interpretation might sound contrived today, but notice the underlying interpretive principle: all Scripture speaks to the revealing of the Triune God who saves. This principle served as a check to ancient preachers' allegorical interpretations.

Come closer and learn carefully.

Do they smell of wine,

> or do they breathe grace?

Are they stuttering

> or practicing oratory?

Are they moved by drunkenness like leaves,

> or are they rooted in sobriety like pillars?

Are they drowsy because of a drunken bout,

> or are they teaching because of their knowledge of God?

You think it's a matter of drunkenness? Yes, Jews?

Drunkenness fetters the tongue,

twists the mouth,

makes the eyes livid,

makes the walls a support for the sides,

causes one to walk crooked, this way and that.

Someone can be stripped naked while drunk and not notice.

By those who should respect him he is ridiculed.

Are the apostles drunk? Yes, Jews?

Was it Noah who built the ark who got drunk, or is it we who proclaim the cross?

Are the apostles drunk? Yes, Jews?

Your forefather Lot got drunk and slept a sleep of marriage with his daughters.

> Surely we, the heralds of purity, aren't drunk? You were right in saying that we were drunk, Jews. Not from wine, as you think, but from the grace of God. Concerning this drunkenness the prophet cried out many years ago: "They will become drunk on the abundance of your house, and you will give them to drink from the river of your delights, because with you is the spring of life" [Ps. 36:8-9].

24. Give heed attentively. It is time finally to set a seal on the homily and to let you go rather quickly today. I know that you will pay your respects to the graves, and honor with your care the tomb of those who have fallen asleep before you. But still, friend, make haste to honor him and do not outrage him. Don't spit on him because he is dead, because his master is alive and makes known to the one who has died before you what you are doing. You go today and strew roses on the one who has died before. [If] you do well, you are worthy of praise.

But still strew roses on him as a spirit of doing good,

> not in a bout of drunkenness.

Crown the one who has died before you with piety,

> not with meat-eating.

Then as now preachers were sometimes forced to cut their sermons short because of time constraints imposed by the larger culture.

Urge him on with an offering,

>   not with a trespass.

If you drink wine on top of the tomb on the present occasion, or eat meat, what benefit

>   have you given to the one who has died before you?

Give an obol [silver coin] to the beggar in his name,

>   and he will rejoice.

Bless the belly of the hungry man with bread,

>   and he will be pleased.

25. The indifference of people! What is harmful we love; what is salutary we hate. How can it be rational today to strew a bed of leaves on top of the grave, and to assemble a public drinking-party, and to make loud merriment as if at a wedding? A wedding is one thing and a grave is another. Why do they exult on top of the tomb today as if at a worldly birth? A worldly birth is one thing and mourning at the tomb is another. It often happens that today a woman goes to the tomb to strew roses on her husband. And she does not strew roses as much as distress him. For inviting her secret friend along, she raises her hand, and the lamp above certain worthy things is broken. And to this the Preacher says: "Let what has been done grieve no one, let the filth of the garment not stain the soul, since this too is the working of the Holy Spirit. It is a matter of water and oil and fire." But a woman like that who exults about her husband's grave and provokes her husband after death — how does she mourn her husband while smiling to her friend? Let us take thought for orderly behavior, friends; let us respect the authority of the Holy Spirit, let us listen to Scripture, and let us obey the Lord.

> It was a widespread pagan custom to commemorate the dead once a year by holding a banquet near the graves. Rather than prohibit this practice, the church of Constantinople worked to Christianize it. This sermon shows two ways to do this. First, they made Pentecost Day, the conclusion of the fifty-day celebration of Christ's resurrection, the occasion for this banquet. This gave the practice a Christian meaning as the celebration of Christ's victory over death. Second, through preaching they worked to encourage proper Christian attitudes and behaviors at the graves to replace pagan ones.

26. Quite possibly you heard yesterday, friend, what the Lord did when he came to the tomb of Lazarus. You as a Christian do the same. What did the Lord do when he came? Did he weep suitably, or did he drink wine unsuitably? Was he "deeply moved in his spirit" [John 11:33], and did he pray, or did he exult and have a fight? It is clear to everyone that he prayed and "wept" and "was moved in his spirit" and "was troubled" [John 11:33], offering himself to us as a pattern for the expression of fellow-feeling. Let us follow behind the Lord, then, and let us listen to the words of Scripture: "Mourn over the dead man because he has left light behind."[2] "Mourn," it says, not celebrate. Celebrate in church, mourn at the grave, and do it suitably, as Christ mourned over Lazarus. Listen to the Preacher saying: "A time to mourn and a time to laugh" [Eccles. 3:4]. Why do they stamp their feet on the grave today, and clash cymbals sounding of Satan, and sing songs belonging to the

> Surviving Byzantine lectionaries do not have a reading of the story of Lazarus (John 11:1-43) near Pentecost. This sermon might hint at an earlier practice.

---

2. Ecclesiasticus (Sirach) 22:11; the Byzantine church used and continues to use all the books in the Septuagint (Old Greek) translation of the Old Testament.

theatre? Surely they haven't conquered an enemy, or overthrown a tyrant, that they devise satanical dances and parade ostentatiously in this way in public?

27. What strange actions! What strange actions don't they perform today, the grave-drunks? Today they design the graves, today they promise to build the tombs, today they spend in munificence talking nonsense: "If I have to sell my hair, I shall not leave their grave without hair. I don't want the man next door to pass by here, nor widowers to walk past." And as soon as they move away from the tomb, immediately they lay aside the memory. Drunkenness is a destroyer of the best memory, contriver of unholy thoughts, a slaughterer of godly doctrines. Let us avoid drunkenness, then, let us show that the Jews are slanderers, the ones who have just said, "the apostles are filled with sweet wine," let us fulfill the teaching of the Lord which says, as we have just heard: "If anyone thirst, let him come to me and drink. He who believes in me, as the Scriptures have said, 'Out of his stomach shall flow rivers of living water'" [John 7:37-38]. Listen attentively. He taught about living water, not about intoxicating wine.

> Leontius works the readings of the day into his exhortation to proper behavior.

28. But some will quite possibly say — for there is no lack of controversy for a drunkard — "What then? Is wine bad, since you complain about it? But if wine is bad, why did Christ our Master turn the water into wine? So," he says, "wine is excellent."

Listen attentively. We don't disparage wine, for it is a gift of God, but we abhor drunkenness, for it is a work of the devil. Nevertheless, in addition to what has been said, listen to this too. The sermon is already seeking silence. The Lord changed the water into wine. But still he did this in Cana in Galilee at the wedding feast, not in Bethany in Judea, near Lazarus, who had died. The Lord changed the water into wine, doing this in the presence of people who were getting married, not in the presence of the people who were grieving for Lazarus. Where there was a wedding, he transformed water into wine. Where there was a corpse, he wept.

To God, who fulfills everything, let us offer up glory now and always and for ever and ever. Amen.

Source: Leontius's sermon on Pentecost is found in Leontius, Presbyter of Constantinople, *Fourteen Homilies,* trans. Pauline Allen and Cornelis Datema (Brisbane: Australian Association for Byzantine Studies, 1991). These same authors have provided a critical edition of these sermons in Greek published as *Leontii Presbyteri Constantinopolitani Homiliae,* Corpus Christianorum Series Graeca 17 (Brepols: University Press, 1987).

Polity Documents

A Decree from the Emperor on the Clergy of Hagia Sophia

To supplement the Code of Roman Law compiled early in his reign, Justinian issued Novellae
Constitutiones — *or "new statutes." Some of these new statutes exemplify the role the emperor
played in the church. He felt himself obligated to ensure the good order even of the church's worship. In this extract from Novella 3, Justinian tries to limit the number of clergy at Hagia Sophia
and the three nearby churches of Mary Theotokos, Theodore the Martyr, and the Holy Peace
(Hagia Eirene). He wants to hold down costs, which were paid from the imperial treasury.*

We order that not more than sixty priests, a hundred deacons, forty deaconesses, ninety
sub-deacons, a hundred and ten readers, or twenty-five choristers shall be attached to the
Most Holy Principal Church [the Great Church, i.e, Hagia Sophia], so that the entire number
of most reverend ecclesiastics belonging thereto shall not exceed four hundred and twenty
in all, without including the hundred other members of the clergy who are called porters
[doorkeepers]. Although there is such a large number of ecclesiastics attached to the Most
Holy Principal Church of this Most Fortunate City, and the three other churches united with
the same, none of those who are now there shall be excluded, although their number is much
greater than that which has been established by Us, but no others shall be added to any order
of the priesthood whatsoever until the number has been reduced, in compliance with the
present law.

Women deacons were
tasked with assisting
with the baptism of
female converts and
probably also with
taking communion
to the sick. They were
ordained like their
male counterparts
through the laying
on of hands and an
invocation of the Holy
Spirit. There have
always been a few
women deacons in
the Eastern Orthodox
churches. The Church
of Greece recently
decided to revive the
order with a more
active ministry.

Source: The Novellae in Greek and Latin versions can be found in *Novellae,* ed. Rudolf Schöll and Wilhelm
Kroll, vol. 3 of *Corpus iuris civilis* (Berlin, 1928). English translations made from the Latin can be found in *The
Civil Law,* ed. S. P. Scott, reprint edition, 7 vols. (New York: AMS Press, 1973), vol. 7, pp. 18-19 of original vol. 16
from which the translation of Novella 3 is adapted; and online in Fred H. Blume, *Annotated Justinian Code,* ed.
Timothy Kearly (University of Wyoming College of Law), accessed 25 August 2009. See http://uwacadweb.uwyo.
edu/blume&justinian/default.asp.

A Decree on Worship from the Emperor

This extract is from Novella 137. In the mid-sixth century, Emperor Justinian grew concerned that the prayers of the liturgy were being said in such a low voice that the people could not hear their content. Making the prayers audible was made difficult in Hagia Sophia by the immense size of the space and by the practice of saying the anaphora while bowing. Justinian issued this statute in 565, shortly before his death. This mandate is a good example of a standard principle in liturgical history: laws regarding liturgical practices, whether they command or prohibit certain things, are indications that the opposite is actually going on, since laws rarely mandate what already is common practice. Notice that the anaphoras on pp. 93-103 include instructions for speaking out loud and speaking to one's self ("privately"), which shows that Justinian's decree was not effective in the long run.

Because of the way their content often commemorated God's saving activity, prayers were in some sense a ministry of the Word of God. Justinian appeared concerned that his people were not benefiting from hearing this prayed remembrance of the Gospel.

Moreover we order all bishops and priests to say the prayers used in the divine oblation and in holy baptism not inaudibly, but in a voice that can be heard by the faithful people, that the souls of those who listen may be excited to greater compunction and raise up glorification to the Lord God. For as the Divine Apostle states in his First Epistle to the Corinthians: "But if you solely bless in spirit, how, after your act of grace, can the layman, who does not hear what you say, pronounce the holy word Amen; for if, while you are offering thanks to God, he does not understand, he will not be edified" [1 Cor. 14:16-17]. Again, in his Epistle to the Romans, he says: "Even though one may sincerely trust in the justice of God, confessions should be made with the mouth in order that salvation may be obtained" [Rom. 10:10]. Hence it is fitting that the prayers in the holy oblation and the other prayers be offered by the most holy bishops and presbyters in an audible tone to Our Lord Jesus Christ Our God, with the Father and the Holy Spirit. We notify all ecclesiastics that if they should violate any of these provisions, they must render an account of their conduct on the terrible Judgment Day of Our Lord and Savior Jesus Christ; and that We, when informed of these matters, shall not disregard them, and leave them unpunished.

Source: The version of Novella 137 is compiled from English translations in Robert F. Taft, *Through Their Own Eyes: Liturgy as the Byzantines Saw It* (Berkeley: InterOrthodox Press, 2006), p. 103; Hugh Wybrew, *The Orthodox Liturgy* (Crestwood, N.Y.: St. Vladimir's Seminary Press, 1989), p. 86; and *The Civil Law,* ed. S. P. Scott, reprint edition (New York: AMS Press, 1973), vol. 7, p. 156 of original vol. 16, with reference to the edition of *Novellae,* ed. Rudolf Schöll and Wilhelm Kroll, vol. 3 of *Corpus iuris civilis* (Berlin, 1928).

PART THREE

ASSISTING THE INVESTIGATION

Why Study Constantinople's Worship?
Suggestions for Devotional Use

The following are suggestions for devotional use that correspond with specific sections of the book.

Describing Constantinople's Worship

- "Heaven on earth." That's how Constantinople's Christians experienced worship. Reflect on your own experience of worship. How would you describe your experience? What contributes to this experience? How might you deepen your experience of worship?

- How would you describe heaven? Where and how have you seen heaven manifested in your church's worship?

- Christians in sixth-century Constantinople lived through unsettled times with nearly constant warfare, civil unrest, devastating earthquakes, and death-dealing plagues. Yet the architectural, artistic, literary, and other cultural remains presented in this book exhibit confidence, peace, and even joy. As you look at and read through the material in this book, ask yourself what the source of this confidence was for Constantinople's Christians. How were they able to maintain joy in such difficult times? How can you find joy in the face of life's hardships? How do life's hardships affect your worship?

People and Artifacts

- In the images pictured on these pages we see various aids to worship — the Gospel book, the chalice and paten, the icons — all beautifully decorated. What material things help you in your worship? How do they help you? Do you treat these things with the kind of dignity and honor shown the objects pictured here?

- Place the sixth-century icon of Christ (p. 34) in front of you. Open a Bible to Matthew 5:1ff. and read Christ's Sermon on the Mount slowly as you occasionally look at the icon.

Worship Setting and Space

- Page through these depictions of Constantinople's main worship space, and then read through the order of Sunday worship on pp. 83-92. Look again at these depictions and

137

picture yourself as one of the throng pouring into this worship space at the beginning of the worship service. What do you see? What do you hear? What do you smell? What do you feel? Where and how do you feel God in this space? Does this worship space give you a sense of "heaven on earth"?

- Go to a very large space, church or otherwise, with a high ceiling. Consider how large spaces help create a sense of something large and transcendent. Looking up, pray the first prayer found on p. 84.

Descriptions of Worship

- In the extracts from Maximus the Confessor, we see a close relationship between theology, worship, and the way life should be lived. Spend some time reflecting on your own beliefs, life, and worship practice. How does what you believe affect the way you worship and the way you live? How does the way you worship affect your beliefs and your way of life? How does the way you live your life affect your beliefs and your worship?
- Procopius and Paul the Silentiary describe a space designed to inspire worship. What effect does your environment have on your worship? What inspires you to worship? Have you ever been inspired to worship by beauty?

Order of Service and Texts

- From the gathering before worship and the common entrance of the people into the church to the kiss of peace and the common chanting of the creed, Byzantine worship calls for unity among Christians. To what extent do you experience unity in worship? Do you sense a need for unity in worship? What might you do to foster unity?
- Byzantine worship displays a strong sense of participation in heavenly worship and of God's nearness. What is your experience of God in worship?
- Read meditatively each of the Eucharistic prayers on pp. 93-99 and pp. 100-103. What attitudes does each prayer inspire in you? What does each prayer say about God? What does each say about the world and about your place in it?
- These Eucharistic prayers are based on an ancient — in fact, Jewish — pattern of prayer with praise and thanksgiving followed by petitions. Using these prayers as rough models, create your own great prayer of thanksgiving. For what do you praise God? For what do you give thanks? For what do you ask? How might following this model of prayer contribute to your prayer life?

Sermons

- Byzantine sermons often place the hearers in the biblical stories by narrating the events as if they are taking place "today" (notice how the word *today* is used on pp. 105 and 125). The preachers call on the hearers to be witnesses to the events described; the sung sermons (pp. 105-12 and pp. 113-20) even give them a refrain to use to affirm what is being said. Imagine you are one of the hearers of these sermons. Do these sermons help you better understand the meaning of Christmas, baptism, or Pentecost for your life?

- Memorize the refrain for the kontakion by Romanos the Melodist on Christ's nativity: "a little child, God before the ages." Consider the paradox of the Incarnation: a small child who is also God Incarnate. Several times during a day, repeat this refrain slowly. Each time add a thanksgiving for a specific way in which God was manifested in Christ's life and ministry.

- At several points in these sermons we sense a continued tension between the church and a lingering pagan culture. Sometimes the preachers exhort their hearers to avoid falling back into pagan beliefs and practices. Sometimes they try to reform pagan practices by giving them Christian meanings and suggesting more appropriate ways of doing them. What tensions do you sense between your beliefs or worship practices and the larger culture and society around you? Do you see similar tensions in your church? How does the surrounding culture influence your devotional life? How does your devotional life affect the way you view culture and society? Pray that God will grant discernment and wisdom in negotiating this tension in your life and in the life of your church.

Polity Documents

- Emperor Justinian made a decree (p. 134) to try to ensure that the prayers at the worship services be said so that everyone could hear them. Why is it important to be able to hear the prayers? What do you personally get out of listening to other people pray? If your habit is to pray silently, try saying your own prayers aloud instead. How does this change your experience of prayer?

Why Study Constantinople's Worship?
Discussion Questions for Small Groups

The following are discussion questions for each section of this book.

General Introduction and Timeline

* What makes Constantinople unique for the development of Christianity?
* What might it have been like to be a resident of Constantinople in the sixth century?
* How would world and local events have affected you? How might the theological controversies of the time have affected you?

Describing the Community's Worship

* The order of worship in Constantinople contained a good deal of symbolic significance. How would using and paying attention to the symbols in worship change your sense of worship? What would be gained or lost?
* Movement, both before and during the worship service, played a significant role in Constantinople's worship. What role does movement play in your own worship? How does movement add or detract from worship?
* Ceremonials and solemnity were important elements in Constantinople's worship. Does your church's worship make use of ceremonials? In what ways is solemnity conveyed in your church's worship? Are these elements important to worship? Why or why not?
* In your opinion, is your worship similar to the worship in sixth-century Constantinople? In what ways? What can we learn about worshiping from sixth-century Constantinople?

People and Artifacts

* Byzantine craftspeople took great care in the things they created to use in church: the vessels used for communion, the Gospel book, the vestments worn by the ministers, the furnishings and artwork. The production of such works and their donation to the church were considered to be forms of prayer. Do you notice the same level of devotion in the things used in your church's worship?
* Some of the objects used in the decoration and worship of the church, such as the

Gospel book and icons, became focuses of piety and objects of veneration. What role can material things play in prayer life and the worship of the church?

• The emperors and empresses had an official and active role in the church's worship. What are the possible benefits and dangers of having government officials play such a role?

Worship Setting and Space

• Imagine what it might have been like to be a worshiper in Hagia Sophia. What feelings and thoughts might you have had? What today would evoke similar thoughts and feelings in you?

• As you look through these images, do you think these spaces gave a greater sense of God being present among the people or of God being a distant, majestic ruler? What features contribute to either sense?

Descriptions of Worship

• For Maximus the assembly of the church in worship is part of the plan of salvation. According to Maximus, in what ways is the church's worship related to salvation? What role do you think worship plays in salvation?

• How do Maximus's interpretations of the worship service correspond with the meaning in the texts and order of service (see pp. 83-92)? Is Maximus justified in his interpretations, or does he read too much into the service?

• What can be learned from a worship service?

• Why does Maximus think it is important to go to church? Why do you go to church?

• Is the lavishness of the decorations and furnishings in Hagia Sophia as described by Procopius and Paul the Silentiary justifiable? What did the decorations and furnishings contribute to worship?

• Is there value in striving for magnificence in a church building?

Order of Service and Texts

A Reconstruction of the Order of a Divine Liturgy of Saint Basil

• What role do psalms and hymns play in this service? What role does music play in your worship?

• What is the relationship between the Bible readings and the other parts of the service? How are Bible readings incorporated into your worship?

- The text for this service is filled with prayers. Is it possible to have too many prayers in worship? Is it better to have multiple smaller prayers or one large prayer in a worship service?
- Do you think all the written texts stifle the activity of the Holy Spirit in worship? How might the Spirit work in such worship?
- In this service, how many different kinds of prayers are there? What kinds of things are prayed for? What do these requests tell us about how this community understands the relationship between God and God's people?
- At one point (p. 86), a deacon sends all the unbaptized catechumens out of the service. Why might he do this? What does this communicate about what happens after their dismissal? Are there people we prevent from joining particular parts of our services? If so, why? What does this communicate about those parts of the service?

The Two Main Prayers Said at the Lord's Supper

- How do these prayers differ one from the other in theology, feeling, and/or style?
- How many Bible references can you find in these prayers? What do these references tell you about the piety of the prayers' authors and the community that used them?
- As you read through these communion prayers, notice the references to God, particularly the different Persons of the Trinity. What do these tell you about how this worshiping community thinks about who God is and what God does?
- What did the community that prayed these prayers understand about itself and what it was doing in worship?
- What do these prayers say about salvation?
- Can you imagine the content of these prayers being part of a sermon? What might this feature tell us about the relationship between praying and preaching?
- In each of these prayers God is asked to send the Holy Spirit. What role is the Holy Spirit to play in worship? in the community?

Sermons

- What insights into Scripture are gained by presenting a sermon in verse form like Romanos's kontakia? What can a verse homily accomplish that a prose homily might not? What can it not accomplish?
- What are the authors of each of these sermons trying to communicate to their audience?
- How are the Old Testament and the New Testament used in these sermons?
- What is the role of theology, the presentation of doctrine, in these sermons?
- What salvation narratives do the sermons present?

Polity Documents

- What difference does it make for worship if the prayers are prayed out loud or silently?
- What do you think about the fact that the emperor is the one decreeing how prayers should be said in the worship service? In your opinion, was it more of a benefit or a detriment to have such governmental involvement in the worship affairs of the church? What does this involvement say about the relationship of the church to the state?

Why Study Constantinople's Worship?
A Guide for Different Disciplines
and Areas of Interest

Christianity

If you are interested in Christianity as a religion generally, then Constantinople is helpful for understanding the following:

- the rise of conscious reflection on the Incarnation of Christ and seeing how the period's theological discussions parallel developments in worship and vice versa;
- Christian emphasis upon the activity — not just the being — of God, particularly as seen in Jesus Christ;
- the importance that doctrinal and ecclesial unity has had historically for Christianity.

Here are discussion questions based on these general religious issues:

- Should theological reflection precede changes in worship, or is it acceptable for liturgical practices to shape the belief system of a people?
- What are the multiple ways in which Constantinople's worship reinforced an emphasis on the activity of God within time and space?
- Why was Christian unity so important for Byzantine theology? What might Byzantine theology say about efforts to achieve unity among Christians today?

Christian Worship

If you are interested in worship generally, then Constantinople is helpful for understanding the following:

- the incorporation of ceremonials into corporate worship;
- the development of worship and especially hymnography as an expression of doctrine;
- the relationship of liturgical space to the worship service;
- the way a strong biblical spirituality might look and express itself;
- the importance of prayer (lots of it and lots of different kinds) in worship.

Here are discussion questions based on these general worship issues:

- Is the worship of your church consistent with the theology of your church? Does it reflect or communicate your church's theology? How?
- What role do hymns play in your church's worship?
- Is the worship space of your church suited to its style of worship? Why or why not? How might the space better facilitate your worship?
- Should a church have multiple Bible readings in a worship service? Why or why not?
- How much time should a church spend in praying during a worship service? What kinds of prayers are appropriate? What is the role of prayer in a worship service?

Spirituality

If you are interested in spirituality, then Constantinople is helpful for understanding the following:

- corporate worship as a way of spiritual growth;
- the use of art and architecture to promote spiritual growth.

Here are discussion questions based on these spirituality issues:

- What role does worship play in Christian spirituality?
- What should be the role of art within the church? Does art enhance worship? Can art detract from worship?

Preaching

If you are interested in preaching, then Constantinople is helpful for understanding the following:

- the ways in which early preachers made Christ and his Gospel the key to interpreting all of Scripture;
- sermons that integrate relevance to the people, deep theology, and attentiveness to the Bible;
- a Trinitarian and Incarnational framework for understanding the Christian message of salvation.

Here are discussion questions based on these preaching issues:

- Based on the examples in this book, how did an early preacher make Christ the linchpin in every sermon? Is this a weakness or a strength?
- Can relevance, theology, and Scripture be integrated in sermons today? Can modern preachers replicate what sixth-century preachers did? Why or why not?

Church History

If you are interested in church history, then Constantinople is helpful for understanding the following:

- the way that Christians adapted to living within an empire that acknowledged Christ after having lived in an empire that persecuted Christians, and how they came to terms with that empire;
- the way that theological controversy and doctrinal developments influenced the development of community identity and practices.

Here are discussion questions based on these church history issues:

- Did the emperor's support enhance the mission of the church? Does a close relationship between church and government create possible pitfalls or dangers?
- What would a Christian nation look like? What would the role of Christian churches be in such a nation? What would be the role of Christian politicians within the nation and the church?
- What role should doctrine play in the church? How does doctrine inform the church's self-understanding?

Glossary

Altar   The area around the altar table set apart by barriers for the free access of the clergy; also, another name for the altar table.

Altar table   The table on which the Eucharist is consecrated before communion.

Ambo   A raised platform used for Scripture readings. In Constantinople the ambo was located near the middle of the nave.

Anaphora   The Eucharistic prayer or Great Prayer of Thanksgiving, the central prayer of the Eucharist. The name comes from the Greek *ana-phero,* meaning "to bring or carry up," hence "the bringing up" or offering.

Apse   A semicircular extension on the eastern end of a basilical church. In Constantinople, the apse contained the synthronon, while the altar was located in front of the apse. Constantinopolitan churches had a single apse, but later Eastern Orthodox churches developed a triple apse.

Architrave   A beam resting on top of columns. Hagia Sophia used decorative architraves on top of columns over the barriers around the sanctuary and the ambo.

Arians/Arianism   Followers of the ideas of the Alexandrian presbyter Arius (fourth century), who taught that the Son was created and less than God the Father.

Ascension   Christ's ascent to heaven after the Resurrection as described in Acts 1:6-11; also, the feast day in the Byzantine calendar celebrating the event, forty days after Easter.

Augustaion   The main governmental square in Constantinople, surrounded by the imperial palace, the hippodrome, the senate house, and the Church of Hagia Sophia.

Basilica   A Roman imperial building, the style of which was adopted by Christians for many of their churches. It is essentially a rectangular roofed building more than twice as long as it is wide, divided along its long axis by rows of columns into three or more aisles and sometimes equipped with an apse, generally on one of its narrow sides, where in Roman times magistrates would sit to hear cases.

Bishop   The chief clergyperson in a church or region.

Book of the Gospels   A decoratively bound book containing the Four Gospels.

Catechumen   One who is studying Christianity and preparing for baptism.

Cathedral church   The church in which a bishop is considered to have his residence or "seat" (from the Greek *kathedra,* "seat").

Chalice   A cup used to hold and distribute the wine at a communion service.

Cherubic Hymn   In the Byzantine liturgy, the hymn that usually accompanies the procession bringing the Eucharistic gifts from the skeuophylakion to the altar. It was introduced into the liturgy in about 573. (Cherubim are a rank of angels.)

Ciborium   A canopy over the altar table supported by columns.

Council of Chalcedon   The Fourth Ecumenical Council, held in 451, which produced a definition affirming Christ as one person in two natures united "without change, without confusion, without separation, without division." This definition was not accepted by large parts of the Alexandrian and Syrian churches, which are consequently referred to as non-Chalcedonian.

Council of Ephesus   The Third Ecumenical Council, held in 431, which condemned the teaching of Nestorius and affirmed the use of the term *Theotokos* for the Virgin Mary as a way of affirming that Christ was fully God.

Creed   A statement of faith agreed to by a church council.

Deacon   An order of ministry below the presbyter, having certain assisting liturgical functions, such as leading the people's prayers, keeping order in church, and assisting in the preparation and distribution of communion (from the Greek *diakonos*, "servant" or "minister," in the sense of one who ministers to, waits on, or looks after another).

Deification   See Theosis.

Diptychs   The lists of the living and the dead commemorated by a church in its liturgy. In Constantinople the diptychs were read aloud by the archdeacon standing next to the altar while the bishop read the petitions of the anaphora.

Divinization   See Theosis.

Ecumenical council   As used in this volume, one of a series of general councils where bishops from the whole church met to discuss and settle matters of church doctrine.

Entrance of the Mysteries   Now known as the Great Entrance, the procession that brought bread and wine from the skeuophylakion, where they were deposited before the service, to the altar table, where they would be consecrated for communion.

Eucharist   From the Greek word meaning "thanksgiving," Eucharist is another name for the Lord's Supper. Its adjectival form is Eucharistic.

Gnostic   The translation of the Greek word *gnostikos,* an adjective meaning "good at knowing" or "able to give knowledge," used by Maximus the Confessor to refer to spiritual knowledge.

Hippodrome   A stadium for horse racing and chariot racing.

Holy mysteries   See Mysteries.

Ho Monogenes   "The Only-Begotten," the first words, taken from John 3:16, of a hymn composed by the emperor Justinian and inserted into the liturgy in an attempt to reconcile non-Chalcedonians to the imperial church.

Icon   From the Greek *eikon,* meaning "image," a two-dimensional image of Christ or a saint used to decorate churches and as a focus of veneration.

Iconoclasm   The name given to an imperial policy, first advanced by the emperor Leo III, forbidding the veneration of icons and encouraging their destruction. There were two periods of Iconoclasm, c. 730-787 and 813-843. In 787, the Seventh Ecumenical Council, Nicea II, condemned Iconoclasm and worked out a theology of icons. This was a specific policy of the Roman Empire and is not to be confused with the more general phenomenon of the rejection or destruction of images, such as occurred during the Reformation.

Imperial door(s)   The central doorway leading from the narthex into the nave in Hagia Sophia, so called because it was the doorway used by the emperor and empress.

Kingdom of God (also "Kingdom of Heaven")   A New Testament image for the fullness of salvation at the end of or beyond time frequently found in Byzantine liturgical texts.

Kiss of peace   In New Testament times, this was a greeting shared by Christ's followers mentioned by both Paul (1 Thess. 5:26; 1 Cor. 16:20; 2 Cor. 13:12; Rom. 16:16) and Peter (1 Peter 5:14). It may have been given at the end of meetings in which their letters were read. By the second century, it had become part of the liturgy as a way of concluding the common prayers before the Eucharist. This is the approximate position that the kiss occupies in the Byzantine liturgy. By the sixth century, men exchanged the kiss only with men and women only with women.

Kontakion (plural: kontakia)   A long hymn or hymnic sermon comprised of 18 to 24 stanzas composed around a theme. Its name is derived from the word for "pole" and refers to the pole around which was wrapped the scroll on which the hymn was written.

Liturgy of the Catechumens   The first part of the Sunday service, consisting of hymns and Bible readings, which is open to the catechumens.

Liturgy of the Faithful   The second part of the Sunday service, after the catechumens are dismissed, which consists of prayers and communion and is open only to the "faithful" — that is, the already baptized.

Matins   An early morning service consisting mainly of psalms and prayers.

Metatorion   The enclosed area in the south aisle of Hagia Sophia where the emperor's throne was located.

Monophysites   From the Greek *mono* plus *physis,* meaning "one nature," a pejorative term applied to those who rejected the definition of the Council of Chalcedon (451) that Christ is "one person in two natures," preferring instead the formula of Cyril of Alexandria, which posited that Christ had "one incarnate nature."

Monotheletism   From the Greek *mono* plus *thelema,* meaning "one will," the teaching that Christ had two natures but only one will, proposed by the emperor Heraclius (reigned 610-641) in an attempt to reconcile non-Chalcedonians with the imperial church. But this teaching was rejected by the Sixth Ecumenical Council held in Constantinople in 681.

Mysteries   The Eastern Christian term for the sacraments in general and the Eucharistic gifts in particular.

Narthex   The vestibule or porch to the west of the church building separating the nave from the main entrance. Hagia Sophia differed from other Constantinopolitan churches by having a double narthex.

Nave   The central part of the church between the aisles excluding the apse.

Neophytes   Newly baptized Christians.

Nestorius   Patriarch of Constantinople (428-431), who rejected the term *Theotokos*, "birth-giver of God," as applied to Mary. He would have preferred *Anthropotokos* ("birth-giver of the man") or *Christotokos* ("birth-giver of Christ"). His teachings were condemned at the Third Ecumenical Council at Ephesus in 431 as making too great a division between the divine and human natures in Christ.

Paten   The plate used to hold the bread for the communion service.

Patriarch   The title given to the bishops of certain important Christian centers. In the sixth century, the bishops of Rome, Constantinople, Alexandria, Antioch, and Jerusalem bore this title.

Pentecost   The fifty-day period following Easter; also, the Sunday on which this period ends, the seventh Sunday after Easter, on which is celebrated the descent of the Holy Spirit.

Presbyter   As used in this volume, the next rank of clergy beneath the bishop.

Rite   Either (1) a prescribed sequence of words or actions that make up a distinct part of a worship service — for example, the rite of baptism, the rite of the kiss of peace; or (2) a liturgical family, a church or group of churches sharing a particular style of worship.

Sabaoth   A Hebrew word meaning "hosts" or "armies."

Sanctuary   The sanctuary is the part of the church surrounding the altar table reserved for the clergy. In early churches it was separated from the nave by low barriers.

Skeuophylakion   In Constantinople, a building outside of the church where the faithful would bring their gifts, including bread and wine for the Eucharist, on their way to church.

Solea   The walkway, slightly raised and separated from the nave by low barriers, that joins the ambo to the sanctuary.

Station/Stational liturgy   The station or stopping place was a church or other location in the city specially designated for a service on a particular day. Stational liturgy involved the use of stations and organized processions to such stations for services.

Stational days   Days on which was prescribed a liturgical procession from one church to another, called a "station," where the procession stopped to celebrate the Eucharist.

Synaxis   A Greek word meaning "assembly," a gathering of the church. The "divine synaxis" is the Eucharistic assembly. In some sources, synaxis serves as a shorthand way of referring to the worship service.

Synthronon   A Greek word meaning "with throne," the part of the church that contained the bishop's throne, generally the apse. In Constantinopolitan churches, the synthronon was composed of a series of semicircular steps that led up to the seats for the clergy, with the throne in the center.

Testament of Levi   Part of the *Testaments of the Twelve Patriarchs,* a Jewish Christian work of the second century after Christ. Scholars are divided as to whether the work as a whole was originally a purely Jewish text, although the Testament of Levi is related to a pre-Christian work found among the Dead Sea Scrolls.

Theosis   Literally, the process of becoming God, often translated "deification" or "divinization." This term covers the Eastern Christian understanding of salvation as sharing in divine life through union with God in Christ.

Theotokos   One of the Virgin Mary's most important titles in the Eastern Church. It literally translates as "God-bearer," referring to her role as the one who gave birth to Jesus Christ as the Incarnate God.

Trisagion   A Greek word meaning "thrice holy," the "Holy, Holy, Holy" of Isaiah's vision (Isa. 6:3). Maximus uses this term for the citation of this verse in the Eucharistic prayer, what modern scholars call the Sanctus. In Byzantine liturgy the term is also used for the entrance hymn "Holy God, Holy Mighty, Holy Immortal, have mercy on us." When the Cherubic Hymn mentions the "Thrice-holy Hymn" *(Trisagion humnon)*, it refers to the Sanctus of the Eucharistic prayer.

Typology   A way of interpreting the Bible which sees Old Testament stories as "types" or precursors foreshadowing New Testament events.

Vespers   A late afternoon or early evening service consisting mainly of psalms and prayers.

Vestments   Special clothes worn by clergy showing their different ranks or tasks in the church. Similar special clothes were also worn by imperial dignitaries.

Vigil   An extended worship service on the eve of a major occasion, anticipating the same.

Suggestions for Further Study

Read these books:

Krautheimer, Richard. *Early Christian and Byzantine Architecture*. New York: Penguin Books, 1986.

Mainstone, Rowland J. *Hagia Sophia: Architecture, Structure, and Liturgy of Justinian's Great Church*. New York: Thames & Hudson, 1988.

Mango, Cyril. *Byzantium: The Empire of New Rome*. London: Weidenfeld & Nicolson, 1980.

Mathews, Thomas F. *The Early Churches of Constantinople: Architecture and Liturgy*. University Park: Pennsylvania State University Press, 1971.

Norwich, John Julius. *Byzantium: The Early Centuries*. New York: Alfred A. Knopf, 1996.

Schmemann, Alexander. *The Eucharist: Sacrament of the Kingdom*. Crestwood, N.Y.: St. Vladimir's Seminary Press, 1988.

Schulz, Hans-Joachim. *The Byzantine Liturgy: Symbolic Structure and Faith Expression*. Translated by Matthew J. O'Connell. New York: Pueblo Publishing Co., 1986.

Taft, Robert F. *Beyond East and West: Problems in Liturgical Understanding*. 2nd rev. ed. Rome: Pontifical Oriental Institute, 2001.

———. *The Byzantine Rite: A Short History*. Collegeville, Minn.: Liturgical Press, 1992.

———. *Through Their Own Eyes: Liturgy as the Byzantines Saw It*. Berkeley: InterOrthodox Press, 2006.

Wybrew, Hugh. *The Orthodox Liturgy: The Development of the Eucharistic Liturgy in the Byzantine Rite*. Crestwood, N.Y.: St. Vladimir's Seminary Press, 1990.

Visit these Web sites:

Byzantium/Byzantine studies on the Internet:

http://www.fordham.edu/halsall/byzantium/

The link to Byzantine Online Sources will take you to The Internet Medieval Sourcebook for Byzantium, which has a wealth of primary sources:

http://www.fordham.edu/halsall/sbook1c.html

Discovery Channel's HowStuffWorks offers a series of videos on the history and engineering of Hagia Sophia:

http://videos.howstuffworks.com/hsw/9421-secrets-of-hagia-sophia-turkey-video.htm

The Ecumenical Patriarchate of Constantinople (official Web site of the Church of Constantinople):

http://www.ec-patr.org/

The Standing Conference of the Canonical Orthodox Bishops in the Americas (SCOBA):

http://www.scoba.us/

The "Jurisdictions" button at the top of the page will take you to links to most of the Eastern Orthodox churches represented in the United States. The Web sites of the individual churches often have liturgical texts and audio files with samples of the various chant styles that these churches use.

Visit a local Eastern Orthodox or Byzantine-rite Catholic Church:

It's preferable to choose one with an English-language liturgy (call ahead to make sure). In the Sunday Divine Liturgy (communion service), the structures of sixth-century Constantinopolitan worship can still be recognized. The Little Entrance, when the ministers exit the north door of the icon screen with the Gospel book and enter the central, "royal" doors, is the remnant of the people's entry into the church with the bishop. (The central doors are called "royal" because the emperor used to enter through the central doors of the church.) Now this "entrance" is preceded by a long litany (prayer) that used to occupy the place of the Prayer of the Faithful, and by psalm-singing and hymn-singing that originally belonged to the people's procession to the church. In some churches you might hear the command to dismiss the catechumens that took place at the end of the Liturgy of the Catechumens. In all cases you will hear the command to begin the Prayer of the Faithful: "Let us the faithful again and again in peace pray unto the Lord." The command to secure the doors of the church is still given right before the Creed is recited. The Great Entrance with the bread and wine for the Eucharist recalls the procession by which the gifts were brought from the skeuophylakion outside the church and through the center of the church to the altar table. In some churches you will hear the whole Eucharistic prayer, typically that of John Chrysostom; in others you will hear only the opening dialogue and the congregational responses. It was in the sixth century that the prayer began to be said quietly. In the last few decades some churches have begun to say it out loud again. The prayer that the priest says when he comes out of the altar area near the end of the service still bears the title "Prayer behind the Ambo." It is the prayer the bishop prayed as he was leaving the church.

Works Cited

Baldovin, John. *The Urban Character of Christian Worship: The Origins, Development, and Meaning of Stational Liturgy.* Orientalia Christiana Analecta 228. Rome: Pontifical Oriental Institute, 1987.

Brightman, F. E. *Liturgies: Eastern and Western.* Oxford: Clarendon Press; reprint edition, 1965.

Carpenter, Marjorie. *Kontakia of Romanos, Byzantine Melodist,* II: *On Christian Life.* Columbia: University of Missouri Press, 1973.

Cavallo, Guglielmo, editor. *The Byzantines.* Translated by Thomas Dunlap, Teresa Lavender Fagan, and Charles Lambert. Chicago and London: University of Chicago Press, 1997.

Constantine VII Porphyrogenitus. *On the Ceremonies of the Byzantine Court.* Text and French translation of book one in *Constantine Porphyrogénète. Le livre des ceremonies,* book 1. Edited and translated by Albert Vogt. 3rd printing. Paris: Les Belles Lettres, 2006. English translation of relevant portions in Heinz Kähler, *Hagia Sophia,* translated by Ellyn Childs, pp. 63-67. New York/Washington: Frederick A. Praeger, 1967.

Germanus of Constantinople. *On the Divine Liturgy.* Edited and translated by Paul Meyendorff. Crestwood, N Y : St. Vladimir's Seminary Press, 1999.

Isidore of Seville. *Etymologies.* Translated by Stephen A. Barney et al. Cambridge: Cambridge University Press, 2006.

Jasper, R. C. D., and G. J. Cuming, editors. *Prayers of the Eucharist: Early and Reformed.* 3rd edition. Collegeville, Minn.: Liturgical Press, 1992.

Kee, H. C. "Testaments of the Twelve Patriarchs." In J. H. Charlesworth, *The Old Testament Pseudepigrapha I: Apocalyptic Literature and Testaments.* Garden City, N.Y.: Doubleday, 1983.

Krautheimer, Richard. *Early Christian and Byzantine Architecture.* New York: Penguin Books, 1986.

Leontius, Presbyter of Constantinople. *Fourteen Homilies.* Translated by Pauline Allen and Cornelis Datema. Brisbane: Australian Association for Byzantine Studies, 1991.

L'eucologio Barberini Gr. 336. Edited by Stefano Parenti and Elena Velkovska. Rome: Edizioni Liturgiche, 1995.

Maas, Paul, and Constantine Trypanis. *Sancti Romani Melodi Cantica.* Oxford: Clarendon Press, 1963.

Mainstone, Rowland J. *Hagia Sophia: Architecture, Structure, and Liturgy of Justinian's Great Church.* New York: Thames & Hudson, 1988.

Mango, Cyril. *Byzantium: The Empire of New Rome.* London: Weidenfeld & Nicolson, 1980.

———. "Saints." In *The Byzantines,* edited by Guglielmo Cavallo and translated by Thomas Dunlap, Teresa Lavender Fagan, and Charles Lambert, pp. 255-80. Chicago and London: University of Chicago Press, 1997.

———, editor. *The Art of the Byzantine Empire, 312-1453.* Medieval Academy Reprints for Teaching 16. Toronto: University of Toronto Press, 1986.

Mateos, Juan. *La célébration de la parole dans la liturgie Byzantine. Étude historique.* Orientalia Christiana Analecta 191. Rome: Pontifical Oriental Institute, 1971.

Mathews, Thomas F. *The Early Churches of Constantinople: Architecture and Liturgy.* University Park: Pennsylvania State University Press, 1971.

———. "Early Icons of the Holy Monastery of Saint Catherine at Sinai." In *Holy Image, Hallowed Ground: Icons from Sinai,* edited by Robert S. Nelson and Kristen M. Collins, pp. 39-56. Los Angeles: J. Paul Getty Museum, 2006.

Maximus the Confessor. *The Church's Mystagogy.* Translated by George C. Berthold. In *Maximus Confessor: Selected Writings,* Classics of Western Spirituality. Mahwah, N.J.: Paulist Press, 1985.

Nelson, Robert S., and Kristen M. Collins, editors. *Holy Image, Hallowed Ground: Icons from Sinai.* Los Angeles: J. Paul Getty Museum, 2006.

Norwich, John Julius. *Byzantium: The Early Centuries.* New York: Alfred A. Knopf, 1996.

Paulus Silentiarius. *Descr. S. Sophiae.* In Cyril Mango, *The Art of the Byzantine Empire, 312-1453: Sources and Documents.* Englewood Cliffs, N.J.: Prentice-Hall, 1972.

Pelikan, Jaroslav. *The Christian Tradition: A History of the Development of Doctrine,* vol. 1: *The Emergence of the Catholic Tradition.* Chicago and London: University of Chicago Press, 1971.

Phillips, L. Edward. *The Ritual Kiss in Early Christian Worship.* Cambridge: Grove Books, 1996.

Procopius of Caesarea. *Buildings.* Translated by H. B. Dewing. Volume 7 of *Procopius,* Loeb Classical Library. Cambridge, Mass.: Harvard University Press/London: William Heinemann, 1954.

Romanos. *Hymnes.* Edited and translated into French by José Grosdider de Matons. 5 vols. Original source: Sources Chrétiennes, vols. 99, 110, 114, 128, 283. Paris: Les Éditions du Cerf, 1964-1981.

———. *Kontakia: On the Life of Christ.* Translated by Archimandrite Ephrem Lash. San Francisco: HarperCollins, 1995.

Russian Primary Chronicle. In *Medieval Russia's Epics, Chronicles, and Tales.* Edited by Serge A. Zenkovsky. New York: Dutton, 1964.

Schmemann, Alexander. *The Eucharist: Sacrament of the Kingdom.* Crestwood, N.Y.: St. Vladimir's Seminary Press, 1988.

Schöll, Rudolf, and Wilhelm Kroll, eds. *Novellae.* Volume 3 of *Corpus iuris civilis.* Berlin, 1928.

Schork, R. J. *Sacred Song from the Byzantine Pulpit: Romanos the Melodist.* Gainesville: University Press of Florida, 1995.

Schulz, Hans-Joachim. *The Byzantine Liturgy.* Translated by Matthew J. O'Connell. New York: Pueblo Publishing Co., 1986.

Scott, S. P., ed. *The Civil Law.* Vol. 7. Reprint edition. New York: AMS Press, 1973.

Sherrard, Philip. *Constantinople: Iconography of a Sacred City.* London: Oxford University Press, 1965.

Taft, Robert F. *Beyond East and West: Problems in Liturgical Understanding.* 2nd edition. Rome: Pontifical Oriental Institute, 2001.

———. *The Byzantine Rite: A Short History.* Collegeville, Minn.: Liturgical Press, 1992.

———. *A History of the Liturgy of St. John Chrysostom, II: The Great Entrance: A History of the Transfer of the Gifts and Other Preanaphoral Rites of the Liturgy of St. John Chrysostom.* 2nd edition. Orientalia Christiana Analecta 200. Rome: Pontifical Oriental Institute, 1978.

———. *A History of the Liturgy of St. John Chrysostom, IV: The Diptychs.* Orientalia Christiana Analecta 238. Rome: Pontifical Oriental Institute, 1991.

———. *A History of the Liturgy of St. John Chrysostom, V: The Precommunion Rites.* Orientalia Christiana Analecta 261. Rome: Pontifical Oriental Institute, 2000.

———. *A History of the Liturgy of St. John Chrysostom, VI: The Communion, Thanksgiving, and Concluding Rites.* Orientalia Christiana Analecta 281. Rome: Pontifical Oriental Institute, 2008.

———. "Is the Liturgy Described in the Mystagogia of Maximus Confessor Byzantine, Palestinian, or Neither?" *Bollettino della Badia Greca di Grottaferrata* 3rd series 8 (2011): 223-70.

———. "The Liturgy of the Great Church: An Initial Synthesis of Structure and Interpretation on the Eve of Iconoclasm." *Dumbarton Oaks Papers* 34/35 (1980-1981).

———. *Through Their Own Eyes: Liturgy as the Byzantines Saw It.* Berkeley and Los Angeles: InterOrthodox Press, 2006.

Wybrew, Hugh. *The Orthodox Liturgy: The Development of the Eucharistic Liturgy in the Byzantine Rite.* Crestwood, N.Y.: St. Vladimir's Seminary Press, 1990.

Index